To

_____

From

_____

Date

_____

Dedication:

To my beautiful Camden Jane:

You are capable of doing anything with your brave life

as long as you find your true worth in Jesus.

I'm always cheering you on from the front row.

Katy Fults

I Thought I'd Have It All Figured Out By Now

A 31-Day Journey to Rediscovering God

DaySpring
LIVE YOUR FAITH

I Thought I'd Have It All Figured Out By Now: A 31-Day Journey to Rediscovering God
Copyright © 2023 Katy Fults. All rights reserved.
First Edition, May 2023

Published by:

21154 Highway 16 East
Siloam Springs, AR 72761
dayspring.com

Written by: Katy Fults
Handlettering & Artwork by: Katy Fults
Cover Design by: Jon Huckeby

Printed in China
Prime: J9588
ISBN: 978-1-64870-913-5

Contents

Hi! I'm Katy.

A lot of people call me Katygirl. I am a wife, mom, painter, designer, and a huge dreamer. I love books, paintbrushes, fresh flowers, chips and guacamole, and sunsets—especially ones with pink clouds. My life is full, crazy, chaotic, fun, and so, so amazing. But it is not perfect. In fact, a lot of days, I have no clue what I'm doing. I thought I'd have it all figured out by now, but I've learned that I just simply don't. And that's okay.

Recently I found myself at a fork in the road with two choices: God's way or my own. My mind raced constantly with doubts of who Jesus really was and is, and I just didn't know what I believed anymore. I had *nothing* figured out. And slowly, but surely, God took me on the sweetest journey of relearning who He is and what He's capable of. He reminded me of all of His promises and how He doesn't break any of them. So throughout the pages of this book, I'm going to share with you the characteristics of the Lord that I rediscovered. I may not have it all figured out by now, but I have Jesus and He is enough for me.

I have learned through this process that we have a choice in how we decide to live. We can pretend we have it all together, that we know exactly what we're doing and all of our ducks are in a row. Or we can choose to live authentically, admitting we don't have it all figured out by now. To be real about our struggles and where we're really at. I believe that when we choose to live authentically, we are letting go of the expectation to be perfect, and we're allowing the characteristics of Jesus to lead the way for us. It is so freeing to live that way.

I'm so glad you're here and that you chose to open this book. I'm praying it helps you rediscover Jesus in a new way. He created you! And He is going to do great things through you—even if you don't have it all figured out by now either. We'll keep growing together, little by little and inch by inch. Grab a cup of coffee with vanilla creamer and dive in. I can't wait to hear how God met you through the pages of this book. You can reach out to me on instagram at @katygirldesigns. I share about my life, my art, and all the ways I don't have it figured out quite yet.

There is always hope.

xoxo, K.

God answered, "I will be with you."

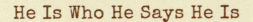

He Is Who He Says He Is

But Moses protested to God, "Who am I to appear before Pharaoh? Who am I to lead the people of Israel out of Egypt?"

God answered, "I will be with you. And this is your sign that I am the one who has sent you: When you have brought the people out of Egypt, you will worship God at this very mountain."

But Moses protested, "If I go to the people of Israel and tell them, 'The God of your ancestors has sent me to you,' they will ask me, 'What is His name?' Then what should I tell them?"

God replied to Moses, "I AM WHO I AM. Say this to the people of Israel: I AM has sent me to you." God also said to Moses, "Say this to the people of Israel: Yahweh, the God of your ancestors—the God of Abraham, the God of Isaac, and the God of Jacob—has sent me to you.

This is My eternal name,
My name to remember for all generations."

EXODUS 3:11-15 NLT

He Is Who He Says He Is

On a very hot morning last summer, my son Miles came to me complaining of a headache. I told him to lie down, gave him some medicine and water, and started getting ready for the day. But Miles kept complaining. Before I could even understand what was happening, he lost all motor skills and could no longer answer my questions properly.

My husband rushed home to pick us up, and we headed for the emergency room. As soon as we checked Miles in, they wheeled him back for brain scans. Once that was over, we sat in the emergency room, comforting our son, who had no concept of anything going on around him. It was, hands down, the worst day of my life.

At one point, Scott got down on eye level with Miles. Scott asked him a series of questions, to which he could not tell us the answers. His birthday, his name, his sister's name, his address. The final question my husband asked my son was, "Miles, who am I?" And Miles answered him, "I think I should know, but I just don't right now."

After what felt like several hours, the doctor finally came to show us the brain scans. Miles was suffering a delayed and severe concussion from when he had hit his head two days prior. The next step was a spinal tap, but it was a risky procedure, and the doctor wanted Miles to try sleeping first. He felt that Miles would come out of this incoherent state once he got some rest. Sure enough, the doctor was right. When Miles woke up from a long nap, he said, "Hi, Mom! I'm hungry. What's for breakfast?" He's been okay ever since.

This happened in one of the darkest seasons of my life. A season when I felt confused about my faith. There was a lot of turmoil in my heart and my mind, and I was ready to give up on Jesus. Looking back, I feel like in the very darkest places of my soul, Jesus was looking into my eyes and saying, "Who am I, Katy?"

And my response back to him: "I feel like I should know You, but I don't right now."

I have a feeling I'm not the only one. With all that's going on in our world, so many of us feel a lot like Miles did—confused and unsure of even what once seemed most certain. That's a hard place to be, but it's not where we have to stay.

Eventually, I remembered who Jesus was and is. And eventually I woke up and realized His way is always better. So much better. But in those dark moments, gosh, I could feel Jesus gently reminding me. Just like Scott reminded Miles that scary day, "Buddy, it's me! Your dad!"

These are the kinds of truths our hearts need to hear, the kind you'll find in the thirty-one chapters of this book. . . .

It's Me, Daughter.
I came for you.
I am your Savior.
I am your comfort.
I am your redeemer.
I am your freedom.
I am your peace.
I am your restorer.

I am your teacher.
I am your grace.
I am the Lord, your God.
I am holding your hand.
I will help you.
I am your hope.

It's Jesus. It's always been Jesus. He is ALL we need. I am so glad He chooses to remind us who He is when we lose our way and forget. I'm so glad He picks us up from the dark pits we find ourselves in.

I forgot who God was for a little bit, just as Miles forgot who we were momentarily. But you know what? I found my way back, and I learn more about who He is every day. And while there is still a sink full of last night's dinner dishes, I'm learning to walk in confidence a little more every day. "I think I should know You" has turned into a confident "I DO know You." I know who I am and who Jesus is more than I ever have before.

My hope and prayer is that this book will help you rediscover who Jesus is and who you are too, one truth at a time.

Prayer

Lord, thank You for who You say You are.
I thought I'd have life all figured out
by now, but I pray that You will show
me through the pages of this book more
about You. I pray that You will draw
me closer to You as You reveal Your
character to me day by day. My hands are
open to You, Lord. Help me rediscover
who You are, one truth at a time.

Amen.

I will be glad because You will rescue Me.

He Is Our Comfort

How much longer will you forget me, LORD? Forever?
    How much longer will you hide Yourself from me?
How long must I endure trouble?
    How long will sorrow fill my heart day and night?
    How long will my enemies triumph over me?
Look at me, O LORD my God, and answer me.
    Restore my strength; don't let me die.
Don't let my enemies say, "We have defeated him."
    Don't let them gloat over my downfall.
I rely on Your constant love;
    I will be glad, because You will rescue me.
I will sing to You, O LORD,
    because You have been good to me.

PSALM 13:1-6 GNT

He is our Comfort

Have you ever been woken up by something in the middle of the night, with a spinning mind and an uneasy heart? Maybe you're worrying, maybe you're thinking about all you have to do the next day, maybe you're just staring into the darkness, counting the minutes left until your alarm goes off. It's been happening to me a lot lately because I've been really concerned about something. The middle of the night can feel kind of daunting to me, and my thoughts can get reckless and out of control. If you're like me, you probably start worrying about the time and all the sleep you're missing out on and how it will affect the next day. The list can go on and on.

The definition of worry is giving way to anxiety or unease, to allow one's mind to dwell on difficulty or troubles. I do this a lot. I let anxiety take over, and then I forget all that God has promised me and all the ways He can comfort me. I wish I could tell you I

always turn to Jesus in these moments, but I don't have it all together in that area yet. I've learned that when I fixate on my fears and let my mind spiral with anxiety, I am giving those thoughts control instead of the Lord.

I recently read through the book of Psalms. Time and time again, David found himself in a crisis and fled to a place where he could cry out to the Lord. As I read through the different psalms, I noticed that David generally started out asking where God is. It seems that David often questioned if God was really there with him, helping him and listening to him. Psalm 13:2 (CSB) says, "How long will I store up anxious concerns within me, agony in my mind every day?" Psalm 17:1 (CSB) says, "Lord, hear a just cause; pay attention to my cry; listen to my prayer." Psalm 55:2 (CSB) says, "Pay attention to me and answer me. I am restless and in turmoil with my complaint."

Have you ever felt like David? Sometimes our worries can feel like

agony when we allow them to control our minds and take our thoughts captive.

What I've also noticed about the psalms David wrote for the Lord is that as he was talking out his anguish and worries to God, he got to a place where his complaints and doubts turned into praise. Psalm 13:5 (CSB) says, "But I have trusted in Your faithful love; my heart will rejoice in Your deliverance." Psalm 17:15 (CSB) says, "But I will see Your face in righteousness; when I awake, I will be satisfied with Your presence." And Psalm 55:22 (CSB) says, "Cast your burden on the LORD, and He will sustain you; He will never allow the righteous to be shaken." In all three of these psalms, David ended with praise to the Lord, acknowledging who God is and taking peace in His comfort.

What if we replaced our anxious thoughts with God's truths? When those fearful thoughts start creeping into our minds, we should be battling them with the actual Word of God—memorizing Scripture and allowing the words of comfort to take our thoughts captive instead of the anxieties. We fight these battles on our knees, crying out to the Lord. God is right there, waiting for us to cry out to Him so He can answer us with His peace. His Word will become our weapon.

Psalm 25:20 (CSB) is a great place to start: "Guard me and rescue me; do not let me be disgraced, for I take refuge in You."

His word becomes our weapon.

Prayer

Lord, on the days that I feel worried, fearful, or anxious, I pray that You will comfort me with Your Word. I pray that You will give me the strength to battle my thoughts with Your truths. Lord, thank You for always drawing near to me when I am feeling weak or overwhelmed with worry. Your presence always sustains me. You are my comfort.

Amen.

Above all, put on Love.

He Is Mercy

Therefore, as God's chosen ones, holy and dearly loved, put on compassion, kindness, humility, gentleness, and patience, bearing with one another and forgiving one another if anyone has a grievance against another. Just as the Lord has forgiven you, so you are also to forgive. Above all, put on love, which is the perfect bond of unity. And let the peace of Christ, to which you were also called in one body, rule your hearts. And be thankful.

COLOSSIANS 3:12-15 CSB

He Is Mercy

I got my feelings hurt by a friend a few weeks ago. It was the kind of hurt that still causes a lump in my throat and my eyes to fill with tears every time I think about it. I've been working hard on letting it go, but I'm not quite there yet. Sometimes healing takes time, and that's okay. I think it's important to allow our hearts to feel certain emotions instead of ignoring them, as long as those feelings don't lead to bad decisions.

The thing about hurt feelings is that they can turn into bitterness really quickly if we're not careful. Bitterness can lead to gossip, gossip leads to rumors, rumors lead to judgment, and on and on. I noticed that instead of believing the best in my friend, I started picking apart every action and only believed the worst in her, which just resulted in more hurt that I created for myself. Have you ever been in that position with someone you care about? It's a tricky place to be.

One thing I've learned is that bitterness harms the offended much more than the offender. It only causes more hurt and strife in our own hearts, creating a sour taste in our mouths and in our spirits. But those moments of deep hurt eventually led to bitterness because I wasn't willing to forgive my friend. Let me tell you something. Forgiving someone not only frees the other person from the wrongs they've done to us, but it also frees us from the ways we're holding on to them. It's showing someone mercy even if they don't deserve it.

Think about it: Mercy is showing compassion or forgiveness toward someone when it is in our own power to punish them. And Jesus has offered us the ultimate forgiveness. He offers us the ultimate mercy. I am able to walk lightly and experience freedom because of that. What a gift it is to be able to offer the same kind of mercy and forgiveness to others.

When my son was one year old, I took him to the doctor for his annual checkup. He had to get some shots at the end of it, and I knew what was coming—screams, hurt, and tears by my little guy. It's a lot for a new mama to handle. The nurse, Sally, came in with the syringes and started talking to little Miles about it, using a calm voice, coaxing him into relaxing and trusting her. She giggled with him and distracted him, and you could almost see him registering the betrayal as she gave him the shots in his leg. And before you knew it, sure enough, his little lip started quivering and his eyes filled with tears, and he kept looking at Nurse Sally with confusion. She turned to me and said it was the worst she had ever felt after administering a shot. She was even choked up herself. I picked him up, expecting that he'd need me for comfort, that he'd bury his little head in my neck and need cuddles from his mama. But instead, he reached for Nurse Sally. A shocking turn of events and picture of mercy. The offended reaching for the offender, embracing them, forgiving them, and extending forgiveness to them. I'm not sure Sally had ever witnessed anything like it.

I thought I'd have this forgiveness thing figured out by now. But I think as we grow, we just keep learning. Sometimes showing someone mercy is not easy. It hasn't been easy for me this time around. But the example Jesus has set for us and the freedom that comes from forgiveness is something we should be striving for. Let's try it today. Let's show mercy to someone even if it's not easy for us. Let's follow Jesus' gentle lead and keep growing in mercy and forgiveness.

HE OFFERS US THE ULTIMATE MERCY.

Prayer

Dear Jesus, thank You for showing me how to forgive someone who has hurt me and give them the mercy You so graciously have given me. In the times when it feels harder to forgive, I pray that You will show me Your way and give me the strength to show mercy. It frees me from bitterness and resentment and frees them from the wrongs they've done. Teach me to be more like You, for You are mercy.

Amen.

As the clay is in the potter's hand, so are you in My hand.

He Is Our Redeemer

You satisfy me more than the richest feast.
    I will praise You with songs of joy.
 I lie awake thinking of You,
        meditating on You through the night.
Because You are my helper,
    I sing for joy in the shadow of Your wings.
I cling to You;
        Your strong right hand holds me securely.

PSALM 63:5-8 NLT

He Is Our Redeemer

Scott and I celebrated seventeen years of marriage this year.

On the day of our anniversary, we spent the morning picking up trash with our church as a way to serve our city and help beautify it. As we were walking from street to street, I made the joke that it was a perfect metaphor for our anniversary. We had just survived the hardest, most painful season of our marriage when it felt like we quite literally picked up trash for an entire year.

When we hit rock bottom and felt like all hope was lost, we (sometimes very reluctantly) decided to push into the hard space and seek help and therapy. We invited a few close friends and family into the messy places. We put on our neon orange vests, grabbed our trash bags, and started cleaning up all the junk. It was our own beautification process.

I'm not saying this to toot our own horns or give ourselves our own medal. Our marriage was truly a mess, and it is by the grace of God alone that we made it through. It was—and truthfully, sometimes still is—extremely hard and refining work, and we owe every ounce of glory to Jesus. I will never stop thanking Him for redeeming us and getting us through.

There is a parable about a potter in Jeremiah 18. The Lord sent Jeremiah to watch this potter create. So Jeremiah went down to the potter's house and watched him work at his wheel. Did you know that creating a bowl or jar from pottery can take anywhere from three days to three weeks? Pottery is actually very time-consuming and takes quite a bit of patience to create a beautiful piece. There is an entire process to it. So when Jeremiah went down to watch the potter, my guess is that he didn't plop himself down on a stool for an hour. I think he watched him for a long time, waiting to see the end result, waiting to hear why the Lord brought him there. And at one point, the potter realized that the jar he was making from clay had become flawed, so the only solution at that point was to start all over. Yes . . .

he began the entire process all over! He started from the beginning and redeemed the piece of clay, making an entirely new and beautiful jar from something that was ruined.

That is kind of like how God redeemed my marriage. We had to have our messes cleaned up, and Jesus was the only one who could do that for us. He took the brokenness and the ruins and made something even more beautiful from it. And what I want you to know is this: If you're in a messy place in your life where you feel like all hope is lost and all beauty is gone, I get it. I really do. Hold onto the hope though. Don't forget the pottery process. It might feel really dark right now, but Jesus will always guide you back to His light. It is who He is and what He does. He longs to redeem His children. To give them a new beginning and a fresh start. To take the ruined jar in their lives and create a new beautiful one from the same clay. He's done it for me countless times, and He'll keep on doing it. Maybe it's time to pick up the trash in your life and let God start something new. Throw on a neon vest, grab a trash bag, call a therapist, tell a friend, and start your own redemptive beautification process. Allow Jesus to help you get rid of the junk, little by little, piece by piece. One day, you'll be on the other side of the journey and you'll realize all the beauty Jesus made out of the junk. He never gives up on us and never stops redeeming us.

He never gives up on us.

Prayer

Lord, You are my redeemer. Thank You for taking the messiest places of my life and my heart and rebuilding them after they've been torn down. Thank You for taking the ruins and making them something new. Lord, help me get rid of the junk in my life, little by little, so that I grow into someone who is more like You. Thank You for not giving up on me. Thank You for giving me a fresh start and a new beginning. I love You.

Amen.

DeFeNd Me WiTH Your MiGHT.

He Is Our Help

Come with great power, O God, and rescue me!
  Defend me with Your might.
Listen to my prayer, O God.
  Pay attention to my plea.
For strangers are attacking me;
  violent people are trying to kill me.
  They care nothing for God.
But God is my helper.
  The Lord keeps me alive!

PSALM 54:1-4 NLT

He Is Our Help

My son and I were walking into a coffee shop recently, and he saw a bike out front with a cardboard sign on it. HUNGRY AND HOMELESS. PLEASE HELP. Miles looked over at me and said, "Mom, can we get this person some food? They're hungry." Distractedly, I said, "Maybe." For reasons I wish I understood, I just didn't want to make any sort of commitments in that moment. I watched Miles scan the store until he found who looked to be the owner of the bike. The man seemed like a regular. Everyone knew his name. Billy. Miles kept nudging me, saying, "Mom. Let's get him a sandwich. He said he was hungry." I was nervous. I didn't want to embarrass Billy. But Miles was extremely persistent. So I finally asked the cashier if Billy would be okay if Miles bought him a sandwich. She looked at me strangely and said, "Of course." Looking back, I can see now that the cashier didn't understand my hesitation. Of course we could bless this man with some food. Why was I asking? We grabbed Billy a sandwich, and Miles took it over to him. "Here you go, Billy. I hope you have a great day." They exchanged a smile and we left.

Miles has never talked about that moment again. It didn't faze him at all. But I have thought about it often. Miles was so willing to help, yet I dragged my feet. I was scared Billy would be offended by us offering him food, as if we thought we were better than him. But didn't his sign ask for what we were willing and able to give him?

It's made me think a lot, about how when someone is struggling, everything in me wants to help, but I don't want to pressure or inconvenience them. If I look back on the last few years of my life—some very painful years—the times that stand out to me the most are when people just showed up. When they came to the hospital room without asking, knowing I needed them there even if I wouldn't admit it. When they texted a Starbucks gift card on a day filled with depression and said, "Get out of bed and go right now," and then followed up twenty minutes later to make sure I did, in fact, get up and

go. When they didn't give up on me when I lost my footing but stood by me as I found my way back to the Truth. This is showing people Jesus without intimidation. Just like Miles did for Billy.

What I know about Jesus is that He never hesitated for even a second to help someone in need. Think about it. Did Jesus ever timidly knock on someone's door and say, "Hey, do you mind if I heal you?" or "Would it be okay if I raised you from the dead real quick?" Even better: "Care if I die for you and forgive you of all your sins?" No. Jesus didn't hesitate to help. He just did those things. We have to trust that Jesus is going to step in and fight for us on our behalf. He promises to work in our lives and use our trials for good and His glory. He tells us often that He will never fail us. Psalm 54:4 (CSB) says, "God is my helper; the Lord is the sustainer of my life." Jesus does not once hesitate to sustain us. I guess I'm still learning this. From Jesus and from the day in the coffee shop with Miles and Billy.

Send the text. Ask the hard questions. Then ask them again. Drop

off the coffee. Show up to the hospital room. Don't give up on the one who is lost. Don't wait for the "I need you." And buy the sandwich. Even better, buy ten sandwiches. That's what Jesus would do.

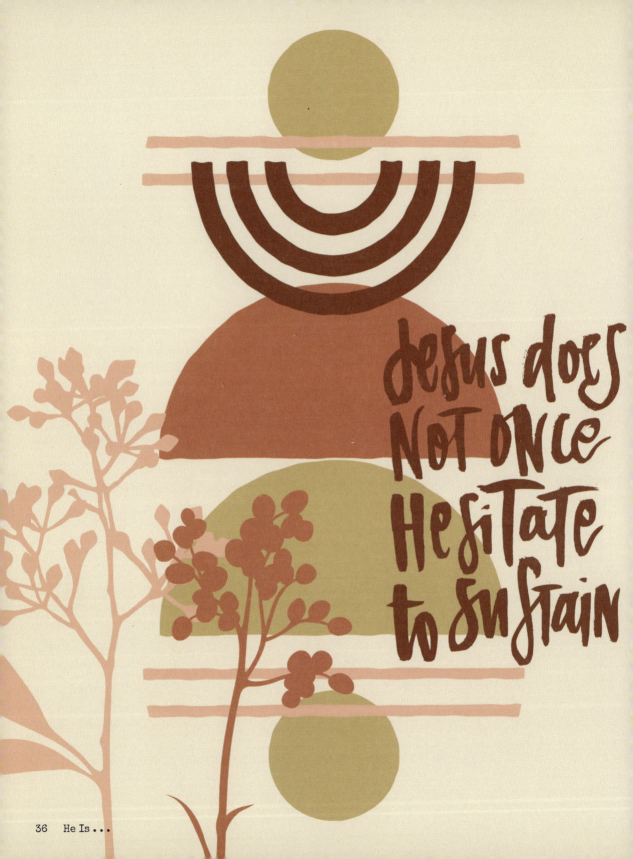

Jesus does not once hesitate to sustain

Prayer

Lord, You are my helper. Thank You for boldly helping me and not waiting for me to ask. You have never hesitated to help Your children. Thank You for being so faithful. Lord, teach me how to help others like You help me. Teach me how to selflessly come alongside those around me who are in need. I could not make it without Your provision and sustaining love in my life. Thank You, Lord.

Amen.

Pause and Reflect...

Call to Me and I
will answer you,
and will tell you
great and hidden
things that you
have not known.

Jeremiah 33:3 ESV

He will restore, establish, strengthen & support you.

He Is Our Fresh Start

Humble yourselves, therefore, under the mighty hand of God, so that he may exalt you at the proper time, casting all your cares on Him, because He cares about you. Be sober-minded, be alert. Your adversary the devil is prowling around like a roaring lion, looking for anyone he can devour. Resist him, firm in the faith, knowing that the same kind of sufferings are being experienced by your fellow believers throughout the world.

The God of all grace, who called you to His eternal glory in Christ, will Himself restore, establish, strengthen, and support you after you have suffered a little while. To Him be dominion forever. Amen.

I PETER 5:6-11 CSB

He Is Our Fresh Start

I don't know about you, but I get this excited, fresh-start feeling in the last week of December. Ever feel that way? The new year is right around the corner, and I just get so excited about all the possibilities. I get a new planner, write down new goals, and start looking forward to the blank slate. The end of the year can often lead to a time of reflection, a chance to look back on the past twelve months and process. For me, the last several years have felt really heavy. It's honestly been one thing after another—a lot of joy mixed with a lot of pain, heartache, confusion, and darkness. And so turning the page toward a new year can feel like a *finally* moment. We're finally done. It's finally over. We can finally move on. It's finally new. I find myself saying, "This year has got to be better than the last one."

And then we flip the calendar. There's the fresh slate I've desperately longed for. It never fails—I get this pep in my step anticipating all the newness on the horizon. Somehow I've made myself believe that because the old year passed and the new year is here, all the heaviness I had been feeling is also gone as well. And while there can be fresh starts and new goals, all the things we felt yesterday are still able to be felt today. It's almost like a false hope and disappointment can replace that pep in my step real quick if I dwell on it too long.

Jesus makes all things new. All things. There is so, so much hope for us in that. And while Jesus cannot erase the things we've walked through yesterday, He can transform our lives today. I cannot tell you enough how much I desperately need His transformation on a daily basis. I would not be able to make it through life without it! Somehow, miraculously, Jesus takes all the hard things in our lives and makes beauty out of them. The pain and the despair that we may be feeling, the guilt and shame over a mistake, the grief and heartache from a loss, whatever it is—Jesus is here to restore, to give us new life. I mean, think about the miracles He's worked! He's restored sight to the blind! He's restored legs to the crippled! He's given new skin to the lepers! Doesn't it feel so hopeful to know that He is making all things new?

I recently painted my living room walls navy. They'd been white for five years, and I finally decided to make a bold change. I took all the pictures down and patched all the holes. When those walls were that deep blue color I had searched high and low for, I loved it so much. The room looked completely different and was exactly what I had envisioned. I couldn't wait to replace all the art with a fresh, new look. But listen. While it does completely transform my living room, those walls are still the same walls. What happened in that living room yesterday still carries into today—just like the trials we faced in December will oftentimes carry over into January, despite the new year and the blank planner pages.

I know how heavy life is sometimes, and I know the temptation to just start

over. But I have learned so much about how Jesus desires to restore what was once—or still is—broken into something new. He can restore our future while also restoring our past. Amazing, right? Jesus puts all things back together while also making it new again. The fresh start, the blank page, the new paint smell—Jesus is it. He brings us the hope of newness, and I can't get enough of it. If anything is going to give me a permanent pep in my step, that is it. I'm so thankful Jesus is my ultimate fresh start.

Jesus is our ultimate fresh start.

Prayer

Lord, You have given me more fresh starts than I can even count. Thank You for continuing to make me new again. Continue to restore me, giving me a blank slate and reminding me what it's like to follow You. Thank You for giving me new life, for turning ashes into beauty for me, for restoring my future and my past. I surrender to You, Jesus.

Amen.

It is NOT those who are well who Need a doctor, but those who are sick.

He Is Our Pew Companion

As Jesus went on from there, he saw a man named Matthew sitting at the tax office, and he said to him, "Follow Me," and he got up and followed Him.

While He was reclining at the table in the house, many tax collectors and sinners came to eat with Jesus and His disciples. When the Pharisees saw this, they asked His disciples, "Why does Your teacher eat with tax collectors and sinners?"

Now when He heard this, He said, "It is not those who are well who need a doctor, but those who are sick. Go and learn what this means: I desire mercy and not sacrifice. For I didn't come to call the righteous, but sinners."

MATTHEW 9:9-13 CSB

He Is Our Pew Companion

Have you ever made a huge mistake you felt like you weren't going to recover from? I'm not talking about a mistake like you forgot it was trash day or you missed school pickup by fifteen minutes (I've done both of those, by the way). I'm talking about a deep, personal mistake that leaves you feeling shame upon shame upon shame for days on end. I've been there. It can feel like we're carrying the weight of the world when we're faced with the reality of our sin and the devastation our poor choices can ultimately cause.

What I love about Jesus, though, is that He was a lover of the misfits. He found them in every crowd. He found the people who just didn't have it all together and invited them into community with Him. And as someone who thought they'd have it all together by now, this part of Jesus' character is something I need to be reminded of often. Jesus loved the misfits. He loved the man with leprosy. He loved the demon-possessed. He loved the paralytic. He loved Peter when he doubted. He loved the rich young ruler. He loved the blind man. He loved the prodigal son. He loved the woman with the alabaster jar. He loved Judas when he betrayed. He loved the disciples when they didn't believe Jesus would work a miracle. He loved the woman at the well. He loved the woman who couldn't stop bleeding.

Some of those misfits had ailments that weren't their fault. Some of those misfits just made really terrible mistakes. Either way, Jesus never stopped loving them. I often think about who Jesus would choose to sit by if He walked into church today. I think oftentimes we have a lot of rules about who is allowed to attend a church service and who isn't. We have a lot of opinions about which mistakes are acceptable to be able to sit in our row and which aren't. To be honest, some of the mistakes I've made probably wouldn't get me a seat in the front. I don't know about you, but most days, I'm really glad no one else but Jesus can see my innermost being, because I don't think people would stick around if they knew the darkest pockets of my heart. However, here's what I love about Jesus: When I think about those mistakes and the darkness that followed them, and when I think about sitting in the church service—alone and in my weakest state—I can imagine Jesus entering that room and walking straight toward me. Letting everyone's eyes follow His every move as He finds the person who least deserves His presence, yet He graces them with it with no hesitation. I've always thought that if Jesus were here today, He'd find the person who needs His grace and mercy the most and sit by them, unashamedly. He is our pew companion.

In every story of every misfit in the Bible, Jesus didn't leave people unchanged. He didn't handle every encounter angrily demanding things from people or pouring shame onto the weight they were already carrying. Jesus embraced with grace. He was gentle and kind. He asked questions and encouraged people and strived for relationship. He forgave, had mercy, and He loved even the lowest of these, like me. He accepted the weakest; He became friends with the sinners; He loved the ones who respected Him the least. And you know what? The misfits started following Jesus because they saw the miracles He worked in their lives—like the miracles He's worked in mine—and they started desiring to be more like Him. I love that so much.

If you're like me and you carry the burden of shame from either choices you've made in your past or ones you're making now in your present, I want you to know that Jesus loves you. At your darkest moment, when you couldn't even pick your head up from the pillow, when you didn't know if you could go on anymore, when you didn't know how you'd ever break free from whatever it was or is that is binding you, Jesus walked into that room and chose you to sit by. He loves you endlessly and radically and is gently calling you into gracious change. I wouldn't be who I am today if Jesus didn't go against all odds and continue loving a misfit like me. He is our pew companion, and He chooses us to sit by and love no matter what. *No matter what.*

He finds the person who needs His grace + mercy the most and dits by them—unashamedly.

Prayer

Jesus, I am so thankful that You have provided a place for me to sit with You. Thank You for loving me at my worst and my darkest moments. Thank You for covering my shame with Your mercy. Thank You for being so patient with me and taking a chance on me. Thank You for breaking me free and calling me to follow You. You are my pew companion, and I love You.

Amen.

Freedom is what we have.

He Is Our Freedom

Freedom is what we have—Christ has set us free! Stand, then, as free people, and do not allow yourselves to become slaves again.

GALATIANS 5:1 GNT

He Is Our Freedom

I am so thankful for freedom in Christ. I would be so lost without it.

A few years ago, I made an appointment at a tattoo parlor. I had been wanting to get the word *free* tattooed on my wrist for years, and I was finally going to do it. That word holds a lot of meaning for me because I feel like Jesus has broken so many chains in my life that have weighed me down. But as the appointment got closer, I remember feeling really nervous about it. I was struggling a lot with anxiety in my life, and I knew there were other circumstances holding me back. I told a friend the night before that I didn't feel very free, so I was afraid to get the tattoo. She encouraged me to still go through with it and let it be a reminder that we have the opportunity to live free in Jesus. I'm so glad I ended up going through with it, because that word is a permanent reminder that the Lord has set us free and we are free indeed.

I was recently reading Leviticus. Have you ever read it? I love the whole Bible, but sometimes I get a little lost in those beginning books because there are so many laws and guidelines written out. It can be overwhelming! But I decided to push through and learn everything I could about Leviticus, even though it felt like one Old Testament law after another.

And then I came to Leviticus 25:10 (CSB). God is sharing yet another law with Moses, and He says, "And proclaim freedom in the land for all its inhabitants."

Proclaim freedom. Just two words giving us a road map for life. The Israelites, bless their souls, had been through a lot. They had lost their way, gotten stuck in Egypt, and desperately needed God's help to get out of there. And God followed through. He split the Red Sea for His people and dropped manna out of the sky to satisfy their needs. And at the end of the day, it still wasn't enough. Israel wanted more and made that known. They complained about everything. And so here God is in the middle of the desert, giving Moses a rundown of more Leviticus laws, and He stops and says, "Proclaim freedom."

In the midst of everything the Israelites were facing—all the laws, the

trials, the complaints and rules, the plagues, every "Egypt" the Israelites carried with them—in the midst of all that, they were to proclaim freedom.

I carry my own Egypts. I carry my own rules, my own baggage, my own shame and insecurities. I carry my own worries and my own fears and my own guilt. And in the midst of it all—in the center of all that I am and all that God made me to be—I have the ability in Christ to proclaim freedom. The word permanently tattooed on my wrist. In every hurt, pain, burden, frustration, addiction, grief—the list can go on and on like the laws in Leviticus—we can proclaim the same freedom God gave to the Israelites that day.

I don't know what that looks like for you, but for me it is what gives me life. I'd like to think it feels like running through the prettiest field of wildflowers, hair blowing in the wind, giggling the entire way, knowing Jesus is waiting for me at the end. That feeling of wild inhibition. That's what I feel like freedom in the Lord is for me. Like every single chain that has held us to the ground, binding us to whatever we've held onto, God

has now broken free for us. Doesn't that feel so good? Soak up that God-given freedom today. Proclaim it.

PROCLAIM FREEDOM

Prayer

Jesus, I'd be lost without Your freedom! Thank You for saving me. Thank You for breaking every single chain that bound me in my life and setting me free! With You, I can proclaim freedom. With You, I can walk lighter, without baggage, shame, or insecurities. Thank You, Jesus. I praise You for allowing me to hold my head up high.

Amen.

His peace will guard your Hearts & minds.

He Is Our Peace

Don't worry about anything; instead, pray about everything. Tell God what you need, and thank Him for all He has done. Then you will experience God's peace, which exceeds anything we can understand. His peace will guard your hearts and minds as you live in Christ Jesus.

And now, dear brothers and sisters, one final thing. Fix your thoughts on what is true, and honorable, and right, and pure, and lovely, and admirable. Think about things that are excellent and worthy of praise. Keep putting into practice all you learned and received from Me—everything you heard from Me and saw Me doing. Then the God of peace will be with you.

PHILIPPIANS 4:6-9 NLT

He Is Our Peace

Have you ever stepped back and thought about what it *really* feels like to be at peace? I mean, we use the word so flippantly. Peace, not war. Peace on earth. We throw up the peace sign in pictures and say it when we're leaving a party. I even have this gold peace sign statue in my house because it's cute and matches my decor. It's become part of our culture, but have we ever really given it a second thought?

I was cooking dinner awhile back. I remember exactly what I was making—salsa verde chimichangas. I was cutting up tomatoes when my daughter Camden rushed inside. She had been playing on her scooter, and she ran in with a bloody face, a lot of screams, and a half-missing front tooth. She was so scared and hurt, and all she wanted was her mama. But you know what I did? I looked over at her missing tooth and went outside to find it. I did not say a word to her. I did not hold my screaming daughter tight and tell her it was going to be okay. I did not clean the blood off or calm her down or get her ice. Nope. I went to look for the tooth. A few minutes later, the shock wore off, and I ran to Camden. I pulled her in so close to me that it hurt, and I called a friend for help. You know, everything is okay now. Her smile is fixed and as beautiful as ever. But for the longest time, my decision to look for the tooth and walk away from my terrified daughter filled my heart with so much disappointment in myself.

I've thought a lot about why I did that. I don't really remember much. I'm not the "trauma parent." I panic, freak out, freeze, shake, cry, and do not remain anywhere close to calm or peaceful. These types of things always make me get this weird nudging from the Lord like a tap on my shoulder saying, "Oh hey, girl, I have something to say about this." This time I felt like He was saying, "You kind of do this to Me too." I know myself, and when things feel out of my control or disorderly, I skip the part where I should slow down and let God's peace take over. I just go around Him and try to solve things on my own. Like finding the tooth instead of comforting Camden. But then I miss

the part where God is saying, "Hey! I need you right here in front of Me. I need you to slow yourself down and learn this from Me. I need you to let Me do My thing. Look at My face and listen to My words. Do not be anxious about anything. Do not panic, do not worry, do not go into shock, do not try to solve this on your own. Be right here, be present before Me, just sit here in My peace."

I thought by now I'd understand that God's peace washes over us and we don't have to live a life of worry. Think about when Jesus and the disciples were on a boat in the Sea of Galilee and Jesus fell asleep. A windstorm came and waves were spilling into the boat and Jesus was just napping. Most likely if I had been on that boat, I would have been seasick and also worried sick, but Jesus was asleep. When the disciples frantically woke Jesus up, they said, "Jesus, do You not care?" And as Jesus woke up, He simply said, "Peace, be still." And the waves stopped. And the wind slowed. And the hearts of everyone on the ship calmed down.

The tooth broke, and Jesus was saying, "Peace, be still." The waves crashed, and Jesus was saying, "Peace, be still." The depression floods in, the grief overwhelms, the shame seems almost too much to bear, and Jesus is right there saying, "Peace, be still."

I love what Philippians 4:7 (NIV) says: "The peace of God, which transcends all understanding, will guard your hearts and minds in Christ Jesus." We can find so much rest in those words, that God's peace is far greater than we can ever understand, and He chooses to guard our hearts and our minds with it. What a gracious and merciful God we belong to.

When you're tempted to look for the tooth instead of looking to Jesus today, be still. Find your peace in Him.

GOD'S PEACE IS FAR GREATER THAN WE CAN EVER UNDERSTAND.

Prayer

Jesus, so many times throughout my day, I'm tempted to take matters into my own hands and go looking for peace on my own. Lord, continue teaching me to slow down and surrender to You and allow You to do Your thing. Teach me as I look to You and listen to Your words. Thank You for Your peace that I can rely on far more than I can even comprehend. Allow it to guard my heart and my mind. I love You, Jesus.

Amen.

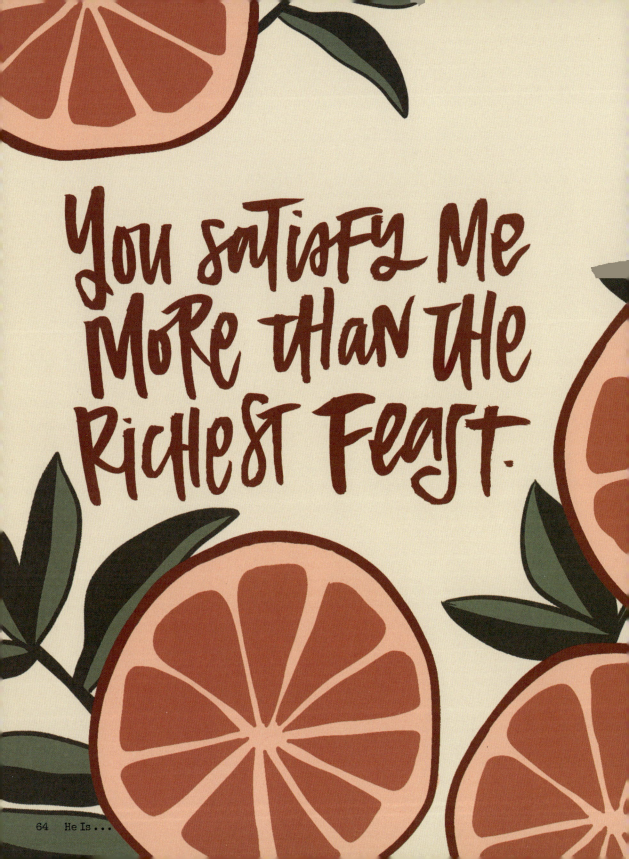

You satisfy me more than the richest feast.

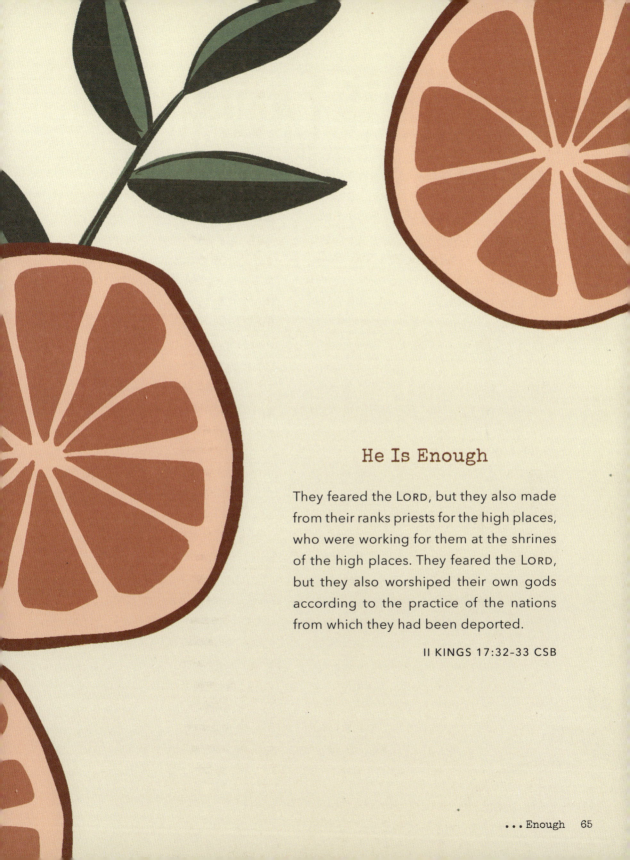

He Is Enough

They feared the LORD, but they also made
from their ranks priests for the high places,
who were working for them at the shrines
of the high places. They feared the LORD,
but they also worshiped their own gods
according to the practice of the nations
from which they had been deported.

II KINGS 17:32-33 CSB

He Is Enough

I recently had to go gluten-free for some health-related issues. I remember when my doctor was initially explaining everything to me, I looked like I was listening, but all I could think about was how I wanted a warm piece of sourdough bread topped with melted butter. I love bread so much and couldn't believe I was going to have to give it up. I've tried a lot of different foods looking for the satisfaction that gluten brings me, but when I'm watching everyone else eat a thick piece of cheese pizza and I'm eating cauliflower crust, sometimes it's just not enough. In those moments, it feels like the only thing that will truly satisfy is the pizza that everyone else is eating.

If there is one lesson I have had to learn repeatedly in my life, it is this: Nothing on this earth will satisfy my soul like the Lord does. Absolutely nothing can meet my deepest needs, my deepest longings, my hunger, my thirst, my dreams—nothing will ever satisfy me like He does. Trust me, I've tried. I've tried all sorts of ways to fill emptiness. Nothing has worked but following Jesus. You'd think by now, after having to learn this lesson the hard way so many times, I'd have it figured out. But I don't have this all together yet. And maybe you don't either. The times that I've truly allowed the Lord to meet every need as He says in His Word that He will are the times that I have felt the most content in my life.

The Israelites tried to live this way too—always searching for more when God was right in front of them. I was reading II Kings and noticed how dysfunctional and messy a lot of the leaders and kings were. They just couldn't get it together; they couldn't figure out how to follow God and learn that His way was always better. The Lord constantly showed so much mercy to His people, getting them out of messes left and right. Kinda like me, to be honest. God told His people over and over that He provided everything they needed, but they refused to listen. In chapter 17, I was reading about all the things they felt would help them feel more satisfied in life, and I came to verse 32. "They feared the Lord, but they *also* made from their ranks priests for the high places." And verse 33, "They feared the Lord, but they *also* worshiped their own gods."

Have you ever acted like the Israelites? Have you ever tried to let God meet your every need but *also* searched for whatever else can meet your needs as well? It doesn't work. We cannot serve God, fear God, follow God, and choose God and *also* choose what the world has to offer at the same time. We can't raise both hands and surrender to the Lord, allowing Him to satisfy us while *also* holding on to what seems more enticing. We have to choose one or the other, and after trying and failing so many times, I'm here to tell you that God is the only one who can satisfy you. He is enough. We don't have to look anywhere else.

Psalm 63:5 (CSB) says, "You satisfy me as with rich food; my mouth will praise You with joyful lips." Every single person in the world is looking for what is going to make them happy. We're all searching constantly for the next person, place, or thing that can meet our expectations. But God is enough.

He satisfies our expectations and our search for happiness, leaving us longing for nothing, the way a meal with the richest of foods leaves us satisfied and full. When we realize that God is giving us all we've ever needed, all we can do is praise His name.

We don't have to look anywhere else.

Prayer

Lord, You are enough for me. You satisfy every single need and desire I could ever imagine for myself. I'm sorry for the ways I look elsewhere throughout the day and *also* serve other gods, trying to fill my emptiness. Nothing works except You. Teach me how to surrender to You more and more every day.

Amen.

Slow down
and remember...

And this is the
confidence that
we have toward
Him, that if we
ask anything
according to
His will He
hears us.

I John 5:14 ESV

THE LORD hears His people.

He Is Our Listener

The eyes of the Lord watch over those who do right;
　　His ears are open to their cries for help.
But the Lord turns His face against those who do evil;
　　He will erase their memory from the earth.
The Lord hears His people when they call to Him for help.
　　He rescues them from all their troubles.
The Lord is close to the brokenhearted;
　　He rescues those whose spirits are crushed.

PSALM 34:15-18 NLT

He Is Our Listener

Sometimes we're just not okay. Do you ever feel that way? You try really hard to hold it together, but it's just not working. I probably feel this way more often than I even realize sometimes. I try to go about my day as if everything is fine, it's all going to be just fine, but in reality, it's just not. Sometimes it has to do with the weather—gloomy days can mess with my moods. Some days, maybe I'm just extra tired. Sometimes I'm really anxious without even knowing why. But it all results in the same thing: sometimes I'm just not okay.

I've learned in these times that holding in my "not-okay-ness" makes things worse. It can take me to a really dark place where depression can set in really quickly. And the one person who is always right there, allowing me to share my heart and my deepest thoughts, is Jesus. Psalm 116:2 (NLT) says, "Because He bends down to listen, I will pray as long as I have breath!" I love the picture that gives us of the Lord, because it's like an adult

with a child, bending down in order to make sure to hear what the child is saying. God is bending down, listening to our cries, attentively hearing what we are telling Him. The picture I have is of a graciously patient listener, letting us share what we need to share without trying to solve our problems.

A few months ago, my daughter Camden came to me upset as she was getting ready for school. "The jeans I want to wear are dirty, and the jeans you laid out for me are too small. I feel ugly today, and I don't know what to wear," she said.

We don't really use the word *ugly* in our house. I don't allow any negative comments about appearances whatsoever, so I was very taken aback. But I know this feeling all too well, the feeling of being insecure and uncomfortable in my own skin. So I attempted to rush in with affirmations, carefully choosing my words so they weren't focused on her outward appearance.

"Oh, Camden, you're not ugly.

You're so strong and brave. You scored four goals in your soccer game last night! You are so smart and capable. You're kind, and you love Jesus. I'm so proud of you. You're okay. Now let's figure out this outfit."

Camden simply said, "I'm not okay, Mom."

I continued telling her all morning she was okay. As we drove to school, I turned on her favorite worship song and said very cheerfully, "Okay, everyone! We're okay! Everyone is okay!"

Her tearful words came from the back seat. "Mom. Please stop telling me I'm okay. I'm not okay right now."

She was right. Sometimes we're just not okay. Sometimes we just cannot pull it together. Sometimes life feels like it's just too much; everything feels entirely too hard. I should have slowed down—bent down—and listened to her heart. She just simply was not okay and *that* is okay.

I walked her all the way to the school gate that morning. I held her hand and *finally* bent down and looked in her eyes and said, "I'm sorry, Camden, for not listening. It's okay to not be okay today."

That was all she needed—for me to just listen. For me to hear her say that she needed a day to not be okay. And it feels so good to know we are loved like that by a heavenly Father who takes the time to bend down and listen. To hold our hands and look in our eyes and allow us to tell Him we just don't feel like ourselves today.

Psalm 34:17 (NIV) says, "The righteous cry out, and the LORD hears them; He delivers them from all their troubles."

What a joy to know we can be confident that when we are crying out to Him, He is hearing us. Sometimes that's all we need—to just be heard.

SomeTiMes all
We Need is to
just be Heard.

Prayer

Lord, I love the image Psalm 116:2 gives us that You bend down to listen to Your children when we need You. I am so thankful You are a God who hears and sees us. Lord, let me be reminded to go to You when I am not feeling like myself. Thank You for never leaving my side.

Amen.

He lifted me out of the pit of despair.

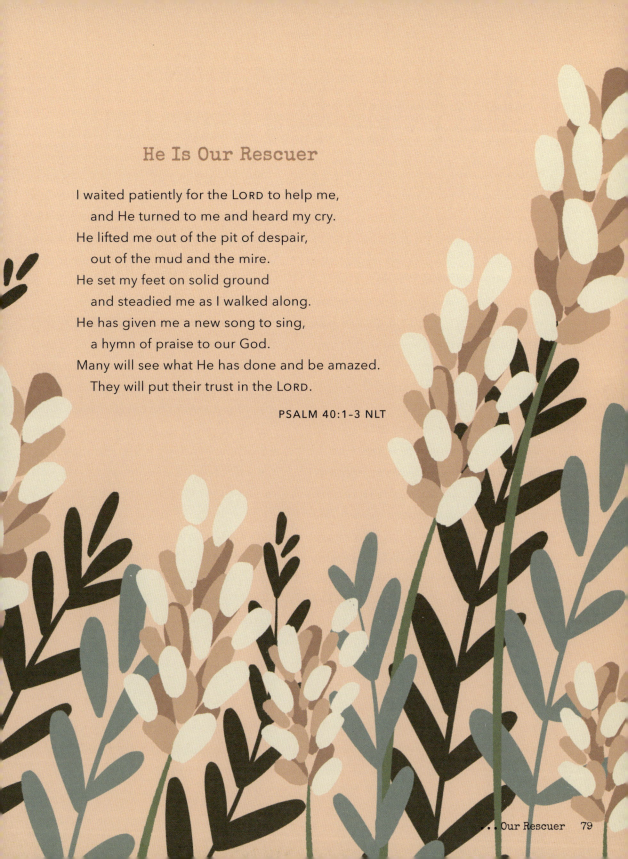

He Is Our Rescuer

I waited patiently for the LORD to help me,
   and He turned to me and heard my cry.
He lifted me out of the pit of despair,
   out of the mud and the mire.
He set my feet on solid ground
   and steadied me as I walked along.
He has given me a new song to sing,
   a hymn of praise to our God.
Many will see what He has done and be amazed.
   They will put their trust in the LORD.

PSALM 40:1-3 NLT

He Is Our Rescuer

Have you ever felt like you're in a pit of despair? It sounds very dramatic, I know, but sometimes there's no better way to describe it. The definition of the word *despair* is "to give up hope." So I would think that a pit of despair would feel like being stuck in a dark place with no hope and no way out. I've been there. It is not a fun experience. It can be incredibly lonely, and depression can loom over you like clouds just waiting to break open with rain.

I recently went through a season when every day felt like this—like a hopeless pit of despair. I lost my footing for a little bit, even though I thought I was confident that Jesus is the only way. I guess I don't have it all together after all. I would wake up every morning very unsure and not knowing what to believe about Him anymore. I would have these conversations with Jesus in my head, questioning His every move and His every promise. I can imagine it would be very painful to be on the other end of that, but Jesus never gave up on me. I started having this recurring dream, sometimes even more than once a night, where I was playing tug-of-war with Jesus, and whoever let go of the rope first would fall into a pit of mud. I would wake up and know the outcome every time: Jesus would surely win in a battle like that. I could almost feel the rope burns on my hands from holding on so tightly and trying so hard. I kept thinking that falling into that mud pit would be so humiliating, but I just never felt strong enough to pull that rope hard enough to win.

After a while, when I would wake up from this dream, I would feel Jesus' tender mercy slowly start to change my heart. I started realizing that Jesus had no intention of yanking that rope out of my hands and allowing me to fall into the mud, humiliated. That is not the kind of God we serve. Jesus knew I was desperate for rescuing. I needed out of that pit, and I needed something to save me from the darkness. I could so clearly see Jesus picking me up and gently planting me back down on solid ground. The recurring dream shifted from a battle to a rescue mission, working on the same team with Jesus instead of competing with Him. And soon enough, I started believing in Jesus' promises again, knowing that He would never leave me. I thought I would know that by now!

There is no one who delights more in rescuing us than the Lord. Psalm 40:2 (NLT) says, "He lifted me out of a pit of despair, out of the mud and the mire. He set my feet on solid ground, and steadied me as I walked along." When we're living in that pit of despair, sometimes it's hard to even find our footing, and the picture of God steadying us as we're walking is such a beautiful image.

I love how comforting Psalm 23 is. It's often used to encourage people going through a difficult time. It's a picture of serenity and peace. And yet, even in the midst of green meadows and peaceful streams, there is still a mention of a dark valley in verse 4. Because that's how life works; sometimes we are in a pit of despair. But listen to verse 4 (NLT) in its entirety: "Even when I walk through the darkest valley, I will not be afraid, because You are close beside me." We can discover two truths from this verse: First, we can

be sure that we will walk through dark valleys. We will find ourselves in dark pits. However, the verse also says that we will walk *through* the valley—which means there is a beginning and an end. Valleys don't last forever. The second truth we can be sure of is that we don't need to be afraid, because God is right there, close behind us. I love this so much! He is our rescuer, keeping us safe from all the unknowns in the darkness.

God is lifting us up, setting our feet on solid ground, and steadying us as we walk along. Our rescuer.

Valleys don't last forever.

Prayer

Heavenly Father, You have lifted me up out of a pit of despair time and time again. Thank You for steadying me when I lose my footing and my way. I know that I will go through a lot of valleys in my life, but thank You for always walking with me through them and making sure I come out on the other side. You are my rescuer.

Amen.

LOOK FROM THE PLACE WHERE YOU ARE.

He Is Contentment

So Lot chose the entire plain of the Jordan for himself. Then Lot journeyed eastward, and they separated from each other. Abram lived in the land of Canaan, but Lot lived in the cities on the plain and set up his tent near Sodom. (Now the men of Sodom were evil, sinning immensely against the LORD.)

After Lot had separated from him, the LORD said to Abram, "Look from the place where you are. Look north and south, east and west, for I will give you and your offspring forever all the land that you see. I will make your offspring like the dust of the earth, so that if anyone could count the dust of the earth, then your offspring could be counted. Get up and walk around the land, through its length and width, for I will give it to you."

GENESIS 13:11-17 CSB

HE Is Contentment

I know what it's like to look around and see the lives other people are living and wonder why mine is so different, with so many twists and turns that I just wasn't expecting. Sometimes I wonder why I got dealt the hand I was dealt, and it's easy to dwell on that. I often wonder why God thinks I'm capable of handling all that comes my way. Life has just been *hard*. We log onto social media and see the best of the best in every picture and video. The snippets we share are the highlight reels. While there is absolutely nothing wrong with that, we can get stuck on the fact that other people's lives look so much easier than ours. The trips, the clothes, the easy kids, the followers, the glamorous recipes, the perfect marriages, the wealth of knowledge that we just don't seem to have. Trust me, I do this almost every day, playing the comparison game. You'd think I'd learn by now.

I learned about this a little bit in Genesis 13. Abram and Lot decide to separate. They were cousins, traveling with their families, and they had different ideas of who to follow. Abram followed the Lord; Lot did his own thing. And after a while, they started arguing. Their families argued and so did their staff. So Abram sought wisdom from the Lord and approached Lot. He told Lot it was time to go their separate ways, and Abram gave Lot the option of which land to choose. He said in verse 9 (CSB), "If you go to the left, I will go to the right; if you go to the right, I will go to the left."

So Lot scoped out the land. He took in all his options. And he saw that one way "was well watered everywhere like the LORD's garden and the land of Egypt" (verse 10 CSB). So that is the land he took. The better land. Lot had looked up and had seen everything the land had to offer and gone that way. He separated from Abram and set up his tent. I can be a lot like Lot, looking out and seeing the glittery flashes of what the world is offering to me and momentarily wondering if that way is easier and better. I think after a while, though, Lot's life became very empty and unsatisfying.

After Lot left, I imagine Abram was tired and discouraged. He was a man who desired to follow after God, but he was left with the lesser land. I'm sure the arguing and the separation were exhausting for him and his family. And I'm sure in a part of Abram's heart, he wished he could have been the one to have the better land. It just didn't seem right.

But here is where God comes in and challenges Abram. In verse 13:14 (CSB), God says, "Look from the place where you are." God wanted Abram to stop looking everywhere else and just look up. Look up at all that God was offering to Abram. It's as if God was saying, "Look all around you, Abram. Lift your eyes. Everything you see, I will give to you if you follow Me."

I think there are a lot of days when we forget to look up from the place we're standing in. We dwell on the land we wish we had instead of the land we have been given. We start to believe the grass is always greener, and we allow envy to find its way into our thoughts. But God is longing to be our contentment. He is all that we need! We can look up and all around us and see what God is doing right here in front of us. He has promised to meet all our needs. And God never breaks His promises. We are able to find true contentment and joy in Him instead of the flashy, glittery options we think will make us happy. Isn't it so amazing to know that we have a God who reminds us to look up and be content in Him?

He has promised to meet all of our needs.

Prayer

Lord, You bring us contentment. On the days when we struggle with finding joy in the place where we're standing, remind us that You are all we need. Show us what You're doing right here as we continue to remember to look up. Thank You for the land You have given to us.

Amen.

THOSE WHO TRUST IN THE LORD WILL FIND NEW STRENGTH.

He Is Strength

Have you never heard?
  Have you never understood?
The LORD is the everlasting God,
  the Creator of all the earth.
He never grows weak or weary.
  No one can measure the depths of His understanding.
He gives power to the weak
  and strength to the powerless.
Even youths will become weak and tired,
  and young men will fall in exhaustion.
But those who trust in the LORD will find new strength.
  They will soar high on wings like eagles.
They will run and not grow weary.
  They will walk and not faint.

ISAIAH 40:28-31 NLT

He Is Strength

I hung up the phone on that day in March five years ago, with the realization that I would probably never talk to my dad again. He had walked away from our family, choosing a new life and forfeiting relationship with me. I've always wondered what is worse—grieving the loss of a loved one due to death or grieving the loss of a loved one who is still alive. I'm still not sure; I think they're probably equally painful. I've walked through a lot of emotions following that day. Anger, hurt, confusion, and mostly abandonment. That last phone call was the first step on the path of grief.

I've thought a lot about grief in this season. It's kind of like wind. Grief never leaves, but some moments are just more calm than others. And then out of nowhere, a huge gust of pain will rush in, blowing your hair all around and causing you to lose your footing for a second as you try to steady yourself. I don't know about you, but those moments leave me feeling very weak. And if I'm being honest with you, I thought I'd be over this feeling of abandonment by now. I thought I'd have it all figured out—how to combat grief and find my inner strength when the windstorm hits out of left field. I thought I would have figured out how this wouldn't all have to feel so hopeless.

The truth is that I *am* weak and I *am* hopeless. I don't have a clue how to handle those painful moments when they rush in. There are still days when I wake up and feel like I slept with a blanket made of bricks because the weight of it all is holding me down. I don't think grief is a natural feeling we were supposed to know how to deal with. We live in a broken world with an overwhelming amount of pain at times. We can't hide from those feelings, and I've come to learn that we *are* weak. We are not strong enough on our own to know how to adequately get ourselves through.

But that's where Jesus comes in. Jesus knows exactly what heartache, pain, and grief feel like. He found out His cousin was beheaded, and He said goodbye to all His disciples. He was ready to bury His best friend. Jesus paved the way for us in how He

dealt with the ache that comes with the unexpected feeling of grief. And what I've learned is that I am not strong enough to handle those feelings on my own; I have to rely on the Lord's strength. Those days when it felt like I was waking up with a blanket of bricks left me feeling like I didn't even know what to pray for. And we don't have to know those things yet. Romans 8:26 (CSB) says, "In the same way, the Spirit also helps us in our weakness, because we do not know what to pray for as we should, but the Spirit Himself intercedes for us." Because Jesus has walked through the very same emotions of heartache and loss, He Himself knows how to be our strength in those moments when we feel hopeless and don't even know what we need.

Isaiah 40:31 (CSB) says, "But those who trust in the LORD will renew their strength; they will soar on wings like eagles; they will run and not become weary, they will walk and not faint." When that wind full of grief comes rushing in, we don't have to let it blow us over. We have a God who gives us His strength to be able to soar like the eagles. I've learned many times in my life that I'm not capable of doing that without Him. Even if it feels like we simply can't make it another day, like we just don't have it in us to pick our head up from the pillow, we have a God who continually renews our strength for us. He is there for us in our weakest, most grief-stricken moments, the moments when the pain feels almost too much to bear, just as long as we are willing to let Him in.

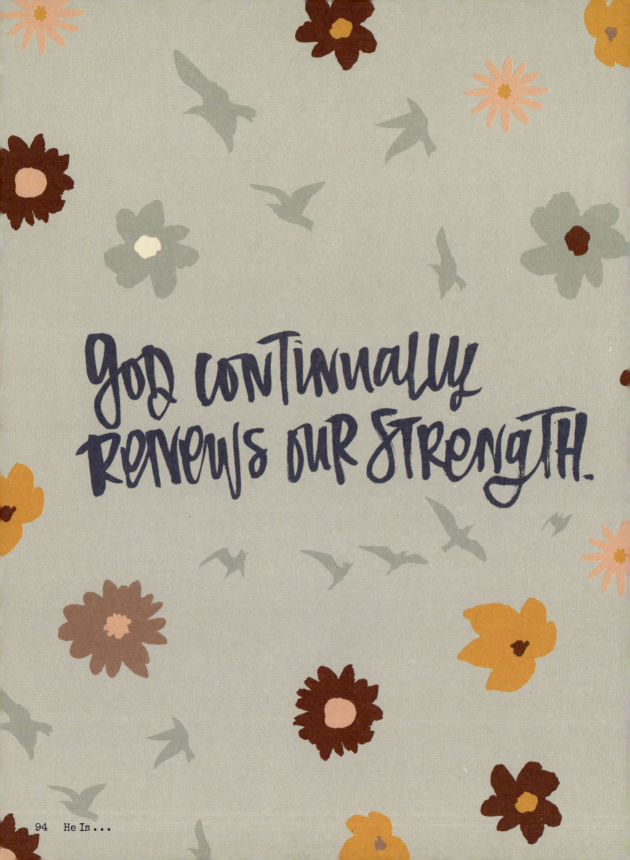

GOD CONTINUALLY RENEWS OUR STRENGTH.

Prayer

Lord, You are my strength. And I am so weak without You. You know the depths of my heart and the ways I rely on Your strength within myself. You know the heaviness I am dealing with on a day-to-day basis, the pain that feels overwhelming sometimes. Lord, draw near to me and renew my strength as You say You will. I trust in You.

Amen.

Better a day in your courts than a thousand anywhere else.

He Is Sovereign

Better a day in Your courts
than a thousand anywhere else.
I would rather stand at the threshold of the house of my God
than live in the tents of wicked people.
For the LORD God is a sun and shield.
The Lord grants favor and honor;
He does not withhold the good
from those who live with integrity.
Happy is the person who trusts in You,
LORD of Armies!

PSALM 84:10-12 CSB

He Is Sovereign

Have you ever gone through a season in your life when you really doubted the Lord and who He is? Sometimes it can be hard to remember the vastness of His love for us when we're going through a season of doubting. And if that season of doubting coincides with something that went wrong somehow in your life, it becomes very easy to blame God for it. You know, it's the whole, "Why does God allow bad things to happen to good people?" question that so many of us ask.

I've been there. After years and years of trusting God and following hard after Him in my life, I went through a period of time when I just didn't know anymore. I had been hurt a lot, and when I turned to Jesus, I felt like I couldn't get the answers fast enough, I couldn't find peace quickly enough, so I took matters into my own hands and just started doing my own thing, hoping it would somehow answer the questions I was having or the hurt and pain I was feeling within myself.

When we step back and think about it, there are a lot of options this world supplies us to momentarily meet those needs. I mean, everyone knows ice cream solves everything . . . for about an hour. Next time you are feeling anxious, restless, or worried about something, take note of who and what you turn to in those moments. I can tell you where I go first: I will open Instagram, I will eat some chips and salsa (my favorite), I'll text a friend or my sister, or I'll turn on Netflix. I might even buy a cute pair of shoes thinking that will help. But in the long run, after I've tried all those options, I am still left feeling anxious, worried, or restless. I wish I didn't have to learn this lesson so many times!

What I have learned to be true is that even in our times of doubting, Jesus is still better than anything we turn to. There is no one who knows us like He does, so there is no one else on this earth who knows exactly what we need in each and every moment. When I'm feeling anxious about something and it causes my mind to spin, if I log onto social media, do you think my anxiety goes away? Absolutely not.

It just gets worse. But when I turn to Jesus instead, sharing with Him how I feel and asking for help when I need it, I will start to experience His peace overtaking the anxiety and calming me down. It is a matter of trust—choosing to trust that Jesus is still working even if I don't immediately see it or feel it.

My two kids are old enough now to be able to wait for my response when they ask a question. But for some reason, when they need a snack, they do not remember what it's like to stop and wait for me to give my answer. They need the snack right now! It goes something like this: "Mom, can I have a snack? Mom? MOM?" without giving me one second for a chance to answer. And a lot of times, if I don't answer within the allotted time they've chosen to give me, they'll take matters into their own hands and get the snack they want without permission, which just results in frustration across the board. Sometimes I simply need a minute to think through my response or consider the options.

I think it's the same with the Lord. Sometimes in those moments when we aren't hearing Him or we think He's taking too long or we simply can't understand what He's doing, we start doubting Him, questioning Him, and eventually take matters into our own hands because we just cannot wait for His answer. What if, instead, we choose to slow down? Instead of turning to doubts, what if we turn to patience? I really believe that we will start to see God's sovereignty in our lives. I believe we will experience His sovereign hand in everything, even if we cannot see it yet.

Today, let's turn to patience instead of doubts. Let's allow peace to take over the questions and worries. Let's believe that God has the best in mind for us. His ways are always better than ours.

Let's believe god Has the best in Mind FOR US.

Prayer

Lord, following You is better than anything I could ever dream for myself. Jesus, in the moments when You feel far or distant, or I can't see or hear You, remind me to be patient and slow down. There is nothing else that is better for me to turn to. Continue to remind me to turn to You instead of worthless things. Your ways are always better than mine.

Amen.

Breathe in
these truths...

I have it all
planned out—
plans to take
care of you...
plans to give
the future you
hope for.

Jeremiah 29:11
THE MESSAGE

My grace is enough; it's all you need.

He Is Confidence

Because of the extravagance of those revelations, and so I wouldn't get a big head, I was given the gift of a handicap to keep me in constant touch with my limitations. Satan's angel did his best to get me down; what he in fact did was push me to my knees. No danger then of walking around high and mighty! At first I didn't think of it as a gift, and begged God to remove it. Three times I did that, and then He told me,

My grace is enough; it's all you need.

My strength comes into its own in your weakness.

Once I heard that, I was glad to let it happen. I quit focusing on the handicap and began appreciating the gift. It was a case of Christ's strength moving in on my weakness. Now I take limitations in stride, and with good cheer, these limitations that cut me down to size—abuse, accidents, opposition, bad breaks. I just let Christ take over! And so the weaker I get, the stronger I become.

II CORINTHIANS 12:7-9 THE MESSAGE

He Is Confidence

I walked into the church coffee shop recently and got in the long line. I am not a huge fan of large crowds, and on this particular Sunday, the line wove around the room, in and out of tables. People were greeting each other, laughing, joyfully catching up on what's new in their lives while waiting for their turn to order. I remember exactly how I felt in those moments—insecure and intimidated. That's just how I feel when I walk into a room. I generally worry about my outward appearance or if I'm going to say something that just doesn't come out the way I intended it to. I thought for sure by now I would be a confident person, sure of myself and who I am. So while I was waiting there in line, I tugged on my clothes in all the areas that I was insecure about, making sure once, twice, three times that nothing bunched in all the wrong places. And most likely, when I left the room, I went over everything I said in my mind, picking apart every conversation and worrying about how something could have been misunderstood.

Have you ever felt this way? Insecure and unsettled? Worried so much about what others think about you that you can't enjoy the conversation right in front of you? I'll let you in on a little secret—this has been my plight my entire life. And I wasn't lying when I said I thought by now I wouldn't have to deal with this anymore, that I'd have figured out how to confidently walk into a room being absolutely sure of who I am and not bat an eye.

What we can be sure of, though, is who Jesus is. We can be more and more sure of Him every day. And we can know that Jesus is sure of us and who He is creating us to be. I've learned that oftentimes when we are having moments of feeling insecure or intimidated, we are actually craving the feeling of being "enough." What I wanted to feel when I walked into that church coffee shop on that Sunday morning was "enough." Like I was good enough, skinny enough, funny enough, pretty enough, or well-spoken enough.

But the truth is that I'm just not. I am not enough. I will never be enough without Jesus. Jesus is where we need to find our confidence.

Philippians 1:6 (CSB) says, "I am sure of this, that He who started a good work in you will carry it on to completion until the day of Christ Jesus." We can be sure of Jesus. And we can be sure that He is not finished with us yet. He is strengthening us, teaching us, and growing us day by day, inch by inch. We don't have to have it all together to walk into a coffee shop and exude confidence. We have the confidence of the Lord on our side, and that is how we can stand tall. Second Corinthians 12:9 (CSB) says, "But He said to me, 'My grace is sufficient for you, for My power is perfected in weakness.'" When I walk into a room and feel small and insecure and wonder why I still feel this way even now, I need to remember that God's grace is what is enough. His power is strengthening me in my weaknesses.

We will never have it all figured out. But we have Jesus. And Jesus gives us the confidence to be sure of whose we are in Him. And our weaknesses—those are things that God is still working on, even if it feels impossible at times. He is not finished with us yet. So it is possible to hold our heads up high and stand tall because we have the power of Christ within us.

The next time that feeling of inadequacy or intimidation comes creeping in, wanting to steal your confidence or comfort, remember II Corinthians 12:9, that God's grace is enough for you, that God's power is perfecting your weaknesses. Rest in His confidence and stand tall. He is doing a good work in you.

WE HAVE THE POWER OF CHRIST WITHIN US.

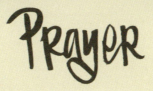

Prayer

Jesus, I am unsure of myself so often. But I know that You are my confidence. I know that You are still completing a good work in me, and You are not finished with me yet. As You continue to grow me, step by step, remind me that Your grace is sufficient for me. Your power perfects my weaknesses, day by day. I will rest in Your confidence.

Amen.

He Is Hope

"Why are you crying?" the angels asked her.

"Because they have taken away my Lord," she replied, "and I don't know where they have put Him."

She glanced over her shoulder and saw someone standing behind her. It was Jesus, but she didn't recognize Him!

"Why are you crying?" He asked her. "Whom are you looking for?"

She thought he was the gardener. "Sir," she said, "if you have taken Him away, tell me where you have put Him, and I will go and get Him."

"Mary!" Jesus said. She turned toward Him.

"Master!" she exclaimed.

"Don't touch Me," He cautioned, "for I haven't yet ascended to the Father. But go find my brothers and tell them that I ascend to My Father and your Father, My God and your God."

Mary Magdalene found the disciples and told them, "I have seen the Lord!" Then she gave them His message.

JOHN 20:13-18 TLB

He Is Hope

There are so many ways you and I experience hope during the span of a day. The hope for five more minutes of sleep once our alarm clock goes off. The hope for a call from a friend so that the day doesn't feel so lonely. The hope for seeing a sunset or buying fresh flowers. One of the lessons I've learned most in life is that there is always, always hope. I think oftentimes when we find ourselves in what seems like a hopeless situation, we wonder if we're going to make it. It can feel like all hope is lost. But with Jesus, we don't ever have to worry about that. Hope, to me, feels like lighting a match to illuminate a room, allowing the light to take over and cancel out the darkness. It would make sense that Jesus is called the light of the world—He is the definition of hope.

We can learn more about this in the book of Ezra. Ezra was a priest in Jerusalem, leading the Israelites to a place of rebuilding what had been broken down. The book of Ezra is about starting over, returning to worship the one true God. The Israelites had grown distant from the Lord. And as I was reading, I noticed how much time Ezra spent on mourning and confessing the sins of Israel and the way they had turned their back on God. He cried out so much, fasting, lamenting, and weeping in agony over the poor choices of God's chosen people. Sometimes I think we need to sit in the realization of our desperate need for God for a bit to be able to really grasp an understanding of how lost and hopeless life is without Him—kind of like the place Ezra was in. And while I think this place of devastation over our choices and the distant place we've found ourselves in is really important, I don't think God intends for us to stay there. Neither did one of Ezra's closest confidants, because after a long period of listening to Ezra's cries, Shecaniah told Ezra in chapter 10, "There is still hope." When I read that verse, I felt so sure of it because I know that to be true of my own life. Jesus is my hope. He has canceled out the darkness in my life repeatedly. I have found that sitting in the waiting is what brings us back to a place of desperation for the hope that only God provides.

This year as we celebrated Easter, I realized that we spend a lot of time focused on Friday, the day we acknowledge Jesus' death. And we spend a lot of time focused on Sunday, the day we celebrate the tomb being empty. But we don't spend a lot of time acknowledging Saturday, the day we spend waiting for what is to come. Saturday was a day for mourning, pain, and sitting in that place. The realization that for one day, hope seemed to be lost. Darkness filled the earth, the reality of our sins and inadequacies carried an incredibly heavy weight, and shame and deep loss took over. I would venture to say that weeping, mourning, and deep lamenting filled the streets as Jesus' family and followers leaned on each other on a day that seemed incredibly hopeless. I believe this day is just as important as Friday and Sunday. Because this is the day that we sit in a place where we realize what life would feel like without Jesus—a day that life feels very, very dark and without hope.

And then in John 20, on the Sunday morning, Mary Magdalene goes to check on Jesus' tomb and finds it empty. And as she realizes what has happened and that she has seen and talked to a risen Jesus, all hope and light begin to flood into her again. Mary ran to the disciples and said in verse 18, "I have seen the Lord!" I feel like it's the moment when she realizes, just as Ezra did, that there is still, and always will be, hope.

I don't care how messed up your life is today or how much of a disaster you've made of your past. I don't care what kind of shameful mistakes you've made that cause you to sit in that dark place of the Saturday—the choices you've made that cause you to continually cry out to the Lord, mourning and lamenting like Ezra. I know what it's like to feel like you don't have it all together and you've made a mess of things. But I want you to remember this: You are not past the point of no return. You can walk free, just as I do and just as the Israelites did. There is still always hope for you, and His name is Jesus.

There is always Hope and His Name is Jesus.

Prayer

Father, on the days that feel like
the in-between, the days that feel
like that Saturday, there is still hope
in You. When darkness feels like it's
going to flood in and overwhelm me, You
remind me that I can walk free because
of the hope You give me every moment.
Remind me that I don't have to have it all
together right now. You are my hope.

Amen.

Because your faithful love is better than life

He Is Our Because

God, You are my God; I eagerly seek You.
I thirst for You;
my body faints for You
in a land that is dry, desolate, and without water.
So I gaze on You in the sanctuary
to see Your strength and Your glory.
My lips will glorify You
because Your faithful love is better than life.
So I will bless You as long as I live;
at Your name, I will lift up my hands.

PSALM 63:1-4 CSB

He Is Our Because

Have you ever been so excited about something coming up that you built it up so great in your mind, only to be disappointed when it was over? That is me with the Fourth of July. For the past several years, we have attended a big party with our group of friends, and we talk about it all year long. We all get decked out in our red, white, and blue. And my whole family looks forward to the lawn games, the grilled food, the melting popsicles, and of course, the sparklers and fireworks in the street at the end of the night. This year, though, one of my children had just been diagnosed with three different disorders that we were privately walking through. And we were at the beginning stages, so nothing had been figured out yet. To be honest, sometimes it was actually very difficult learning how to parent during this new season. So as the party neared, I tried to go in with an open mind, but at the end of the day, when every sparkler was sparked and every firework was shot, I cried big, hot, defeated tears on my bed.

Ever been there? The big, exciting thing you've looked forward to for weeks is over and it just didn't go as planned. Yeah, that was me that night. It was an incredibly long parenting day, an exhausting one, sometimes even embarrassing. And a lot of times, when you have a child with different needs, being a mom can feel incredibly lonely. Gosh, it can just be the loneliest. I used to think that by now in my parenting journey, I'd have it all together as a mom, knowing for the most part what I'm doing, but I just don't. It's very tempting to put on that persona, but truthfully I don't have a clue. Sometimes I want to shake my fist at God. Life has been really heavy for me for so long—wasn't it supposed to get easier soon? How on earth does God think I can handle all this? I'm sure I'm not the only one who must feel these things. When is enough going to be enough, Lord?

I've heard a lot of these same cries before. David shared the same words in Psalms when he was going through trial after trial. He would wake up early enough to surrender his day to the Lord, praying for strength and mercy, praying that God would reveal Himself

to David. "How long, LORD? Will You forget me forever? How long will You hide Your face from me?" he cried in Psalm 13 (CSB). David prayed over and over again that God would lead him in wisdom and discernment. It was all David knew to do.

One of my favorite verses in the Bible is Psalm 63:1-3. David says, "God, You are my God; I eagerly seek You. I thirst for You, my body faints for You in a land that is dry, desolate and without water. So I gaze on You in the sanctuary to see Your strength and Your glory. My lips will glorify You, because Your faithful love is better than life" (CSB). Here's what I love about this Scripture: David cries out to the Lord in a time when his life feels dry and empty, without anything quenching his thirst. All he knows to do is to keep longing for God. And even though David is in this desolate season in his life, he keeps seeking God, he keeps his gaze on the Lord, glorifying Him with his words and his praises *because* he knows God's faithful love is better than life.

Because. Don't miss that word. *Because* we know God's love is so much better than life, we keep praying. *Because* we know who God is in our lives and how He has changed us. *Because* God is a gracious and loving Father. We don't have to have it all together. We never will. Not as a parent, not as a person. But the only way I know to make it is to live a life surrendered to the Lord. Even when I want to shake my hand at Him or when I don't understand Him or when I cry big, hot, defeated tears on my bed at the end of a long day. *Because* I know that God's love is better than anything else, His faithful love is bigger than life, I will keep praising His name and my lips will keep glorifying Him, no matter how dry or desolate life may seem. I may not have it all figured out yet, but I can keep praising Him anyway *because* of His strength and His glory and all He continues to do for me. That is better than any Fourth of July party, if you ask me.

Because of His strength and His glory

Prayer

Heavenly Father, You are my because. You lead me in wisdom and discernment as I seek You. Because I know that Your love is better than life, I will keep following hard after You. I will keep praising Your name even when I feel like I don't have it all figured out yet. Thank You for Your gentle reminders of this when I struggle to remember. I love You.

Amen.

You know me inside and out.

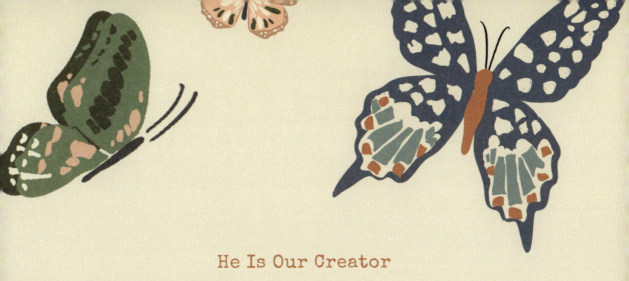

He Is Our Creator

Oh yes, You shaped me first inside, then out;
  You formed me in my mother's womb.
I thank You, High God—You're breathtaking!
  Body and soul, I am marvelously made!
  I worship in adoration—what a creation!
You know me inside and out,
  You know every bone in my body;
You know exactly how I was made, bit by bit,
  how I was sculpted from nothing into something.
Like an open book, you watched me grow from conception to birth;
  all the stages of my life were spread out before You,
The days of my life all prepared
  before I'd even lived one day.

PSALM 139:13-16 THE MESSAGE

He Is Our Creator

I'm guessing the reason you picked up this book is because you probably thought you'd have it all together by now, but you're realizing that you don't. Don't worry, you're in good company. I certainly do not have it all figured out by now either. I wish I could tell you that all my dishes are put away, but truthfully, the last time I looked, there were about eight cups in the kitchen sink, waiting to be put in the dishwasher. I also wish I could tell you that I already emptied my suitcase from my weekend away, but alas, it is still on my bedroom floor waiting to be unpacked. And don't you dare look at my baseboards! Those things have a layer of dust so thick we could make a new rug out of it.

It's not that I don't want to be more organized. I do, I really do. But that's just not how I was made. I have to work really hard to make sure everything stays on track. It does not come easy for me. Is there an area of your life in which you feel the same way? There are a lot of times that I can get really down on myself and start comparing my weaknesses with other people's

strengths. But you know what? That's not going to get me very far. I'm learning to love who I am, and it's been a journey to get me to this place. I always tell people my house might not be spotlessly clean when you come over, but I'll cook you a delicious meal to make up for it. I think it's important to know what our strengths are because it helps us have a sense of confidence in who Jesus wants us to be.

Something I've learned about myself is that a lack of confidence in the Lord and the way He created me—all my strengths, weaknesses, and idiosyncrasies that make me who I am—can oftentimes lead to a place of discontentment and insecurity in myself, which then, in turn, can fester jealousy and envy within my heart. Has that ever happened to you? When I'm in a place of extreme insecurity within myself and I've forgotten all the beautiful ways God created me to be me, I start longing to be more like others. And even worse, it could easily lead to sin when I start picking apart people I'm envious of because it makes

me feel better about myself. Truthfully, this happens to me more than I'd like to admit. I thought I'd have this area of my life figured out by now.

Here's the deal. I think we put a lot of pressure on ourselves to live up to what the world thinks "having it all together" means. But the truth is, I believe we have it all together when we start to realize that who we are in Christ is far more important than who we are in the world's eyes. We can try all we want to fit the standards others see for us, but if we're being honest, we never will. It will leave us longing for what really matters—and that is the approval of Jesus. Only Jesus can fill that void. He created us in His image. All the complex pieces of who we are is what He wanted for us.

So listen, sister. I think we should make a pact. When we're having a moment when we're down on ourselves for not being more easygoing or more athletic or, if you're like me, more organized and less "head in the clouds," whatever it is that causes us to feel like we just don't have it all together, I think

we need to start giving ourselves a pep talk to turn those negative feelings into positive affirmations. We need to start remembering who we are in Christ and *only* Christ. We are His daughters, we were thoughtfully created, we were beautifully made, we are messy people who are saved by grace, we are forgiven, we are fought for, we are loved, and we are set free. Those are the kinds of truths we need to be able to love who we *really* are.

We Need to Start Remembering Who We Are in Christ.

Prayer

Lord, I do not have it all together, and sometimes the ways I fall short can cause insecurity within myself. I forget who You have created me to be. On the days that I put pressure on myself to live up to what the world desires from me, remind me that who I am in Christ is far more important than anything else. You are my Creator, and all I need to remember is who I am in You. **Amen.**

We're looking to you.

He Is Our Guide

And now it's happened: men from Ammon, Moab, and Mount Seir have shown up. You didn't let Israel touch them when we got here at first—we detoured around them and didn't lay a hand on them. And now they've come to kick us out of the country you gave us. O dear God, won't You take care of them? We're helpless before this vandal horde ready to attack us. We don't know what to do; we're looking to You.

II CHRONICLES 20:10-12 THE MESSAGE

He Is Our Guide

I'm not proud of how much I've been worrying lately. I'm not usually like this—a worrier, I mean. I don't like the way anxious thoughts make me feel, like something is spinning out of control and I can't help it or stop it. My heart starts beating fast, I start to sweat, and I can't sit still anymore. I felt like that this morning as I was thinking about all I had to get done today and how I was going to make ends meet with finances this month. I was worried about my kids and worried about some of my friendships. I even worried about what to make for dinner tonight. One thing leads to another, and all of a sudden I'm worried about what to buy my mom for Christmas next year or how much longer I have left with my dog. All joking aside, worry like that can cause me to shut down and forget how to trust in the Lord. I forget He is guiding me every step of the way. I don't have that part figured out yet.

Are you a worrier? I'm sure I'm not the only one. I've noticed that when I get into phases and seasons of worry, I start to try to take matters into my own hands. If I can't have all the big things in life all figured out by now, then I definitely want the small things under control. It makes me feel like I kind of have my ducks in a row. But when it really comes down to it, I'm not praying about things or seeking God's peace in my day. I'm just trying to handle everything on my own, which never really works out well for me, if I'm being honest.

I was reading II Chronicles recently and came across chapter 20. King Jehoshaphat was leading Israel back into battle. He was tired, he felt defeated, and he was in a state of distress over what was going to happen next. Kind of like me with my worry. In a moment of fear, he turned to God and simply prayed in verse 12 (CSB), "We

do not know what to do, but we look to You." Such a simple prayer, but it speaks volumes.

It's kind of like looking at a map, you know? Or these days, we pull up an app on our phone and punch in the address of our destination. I have a terrible sense of direction, so I depend on those directions to lead me to the place I'm trying to get to. And I trust them. I trust that when I enter the address into my app, it's going to take me exactly where I need to go. Most of the time, I don't even think twice. I let the map guide my way. I don't know if you've ever been in a similar season of deep worry, but I'm learning to do this with the Lord as well, just like Jehoshaphat did. We need to let God guide us through all the hills and curves and show us the way. Letting the Lord guide our way quiets our souls down and helps us to surrender our need for control to the Lord. Allowing the Lord to guide

us helps us be still and calm because we're following the Lord's lead, and His way is always better than ours.

And sometimes, when I don't have any of the answers and I'm having a hard time trusting that His plan is perfect, all I know to say is the same thing Jehoshaphat said: "Jesus, I simply don't know what to do. So I look to You." He didn't fail Jehoshaphat, and He is not going to fail us either.

His way is always better than ou[r]

Prayer

Lord, You are my guide. You are the map of my life, guiding me in the direction You want me to go. So many times, I am like Jehoshaphat, not knowing where to turn next, but You remind me that when I'm having a hard time knowing what to do, I can look to You. I surrender to You, letting You lead, trusting that Your way is always better than my own.

Amen.

Pause and Reflect...

You have said,
"Seek My face."
My heart says
to you, "Your
face, LORD, do
I seek."

Psalm 27:8 ESV

He Is the Breath in Our Lungs

I bless GOD every chance I get;
my lungs expand with His praise.
I live and breathe GOD;
if things aren't going well, hear this and be happy:
Join me in spreading the news;
together let's get the word out.
GOD met me more than halfway,
He freed me from my anxious fears.

PSALM 34:1-4 THE MESSAGE

He Is The Breath In Our Lungs

On December 1, 2020, my alarm went off, waking me up for my morning run. I got dressed, turned on my music, and started running. Then, four houses down, I realized how miserable my body felt. I barely had the energy to turn around and walk home. I crawled right back into bed and knew something was very, very wrong. Sure enough, I tested positive for Covid-19 that day. It was the worst two weeks of my life. I was secluded to my bedroom, away from my family for seventeen days straight, as my case was alarmingly worse than normal. I am so thankful I was spared from the hospital and that it wasn't even worse for me.

I noticed two things about this virus and how it affected my body. The first thing I noticed was how bad my skin hurt. It felt like spikes on my skin! Everything was sensitive to the touch, and everything hurt. I've never experienced anything like it. My skin felt fragile, like it was going to break. It has reminded me that life is like that sometimes.

Unless you really knew me, you had no idea that I was experiencing so much pain on my body. We can look normal and talk normal, while inside we sometimes don't feel normal. Sometimes things just feel really sensitive to the touch. Sometimes joy feels far and fear feels close, and sometimes there is no light at the end of the tunnel. We are all facing some sort of battle, and I learned through this experience that no one can really tell from the outside what it is. We are all a little sensitive to the touch.

The second thing I noticed was how much this virus wreaked havoc on my lungs. The truth is that I have not been able to take a deep breath since that positive test came through. My lungs are damaged now, and they haven't been the same since. I honestly feel it every single day. The ironic thing is that when we're stressed or worried, we're told to take a deep breath. For some reason, breathing deeply always feels like a good solution when panic starts to arise. However, it oftentimes feels like everywhere we turn, panic is starting to arise. I don't know about

you, but my heart rate goes up a little higher every time I turn on the news or open up social media. No matter where we are in life, I feel like lately we're all just one second away from having to take a deep breath.

But sometimes it just feels like it's hard to breathe. Some days my lungs just feel tight, and my breath just feels thin. Can you relate?

I don't know what is causing you to have shallow breaths today. I don't know what is causing panic inside of you to result in short spurts of unsatisfying breathing that leaves you only wanting something a little deeper. I don't know what is causing you to be a little bit sensitive to the touch. But what I want you to know is that you are not alone. I can name off the top of my head several moments today when I've had to slow down long enough to just breathe because panic is right there underneath the surface. I thought by now I'd have it all together in this area, but I'm still learning.

Here's where I take comfort. Genesis 2:7 (THE MESSAGE) says, "GOD formed Man out of dirt from the ground

and blew into his nostrils the breath of life. The man came alive—a living soul!" When you step back and think about it, we are breathing the actual breath of God. He gave us life from His breath. So when we are at a place where breathing feels difficult and panic feels near, we can rest in the fact that God's breath will fill our lungs with just the amount of air that we need. Eventually He will calm us and cause the panic to subside. And that is all we need to keep going. We can slow down and breathe easily because of the Lord.

I don't know where I'd be without God's breath in my lungs, but I'm sure glad I have it.

god's breath will fill
our lungs with just
the amount of
air that we need.

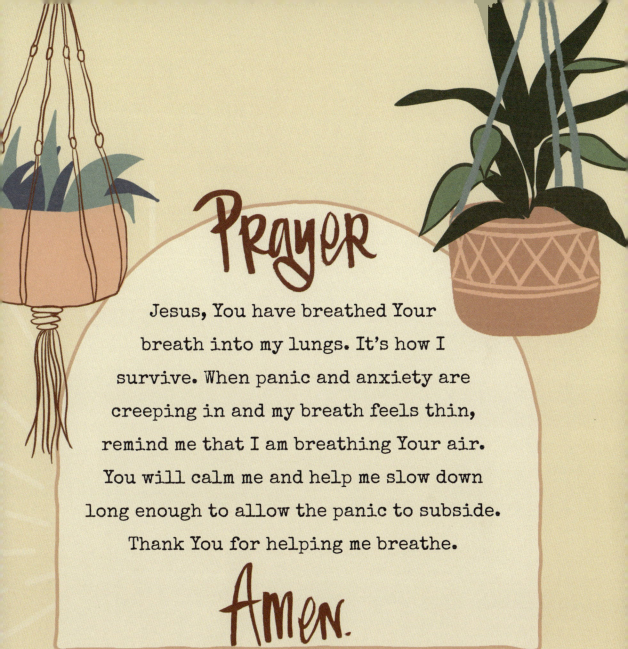

Prayer

Jesus, You have breathed Your breath into my lungs. It's how I survive. When panic and anxiety are creeping in and my breath feels thin, remind me that I am breathing Your air. You will calm me and help me slow down long enough to allow the panic to subside. Thank You for helping me breathe.

Amen.

THE LORD HAS GIVEN YOU THE CITY.

He Is Our Trumpet Blower

Early on the seventh day, they started at dawn and marched around the city seven times in the same way. That was the only day they marched around the city seven times. After the seventh time, the priests blew the rams' horns, and Joshua said to the troops, "Shout! For the LORD has given you the city. But the city and everything in it are set apart to the LORD for destruction. Only Rahab the prostitute and everyone with her in the house will live, because she hid the messengers we sent. But keep yourselves from the things set apart, or you will be set apart for destruction. If you take any of those things, you will set apart the camp of Israel for destruction and make trouble for it. For all the silver and gold, and the articles of bronze and iron, are dedicated to the LORD and must go into the LORD's treasury."

So the troops shouted, and the rams' horns sounded. When they heard the blast of the ram's horn, the troops gave a great shout, and the wall collapsed. The troops advanced into the city, each man straight ahead, and they captured the city. They completely destroyed everything in the city with the sword—every man and woman, both young and old, and every ox, sheep, and donkey.

JOSHUA 6:15-21 CSB

He Is Our Trumpet Blower

You know what I love about the story of Jericho? I love that God had the opportunity to fix everything with one word, but He didn't. He walked the Israelites through every step of the way. I don't know about you, but I heard this story in Sunday school often while growing up. Usually the teacher would act it out on one of those cool felt boards. I used to love those things! Reading the story of Jericho as an adult struck a different chord in me. As I started thinking about it, I realized that maybe it hits differently now because I do a really good job of building walls of protection around myself when I'm facing my own battle.

The story of Jericho is told to us in Joshua 6. The Israelites wanted to enter the city, but the walls and gates were so strongly locked up that no one could leave or enter. When Joshua inquired of the Lord how to get in, the Lord told Joshua that He was going to hand Jericho over to him, but Joshua and his armies were going to have to put in some work first. They would have to march around the city walls with the entire army once a day for six days. Seven priests would carry seven trumpets around the walls. And on the seventh day, the Israelites were to march around the city seven times while the priests blew the trumpets. And when they did that and followed the Lord's instructions, the walls of Jericho would come crashing down and the troops would advance, marching straight ahead.

When I read that story recently, I started wondering why God chose to drag this process out for seven days instead of one. Seven days of excruciatingly difficult work to get their end result. Seven days of marching. Seven days of leg pains, sore feet, headaches, complaints, frustration, impatience, tears, exhaustion, and most likely, seven days of wanting to give up. God had the power to fight this battle immediately and allow those walls to come crashing down without one step around those city gates, but instead he told Joshua to get his troops and march. For seven days. I'm sure every single day those men were scouting those walls, looking for the first sign of loose bricks and cracks, only to be disappointed. Why keep going with no signs of progress?

But then the seventh day came. They marched around those city limits and then sounded the trumpet seven times each. And those walls came barreling down. The Israelites shouted with all their might, advancing straight ahead, capturing the city of Jericho. God knew the whole time exactly what would happen—that those men would win that battle—but He had a plan. And when everything seemed absolutely impossible, God knew that on the seventh day, the walls would lose their stronghold. This is where the hard work comes in. I believe God knew how far the Israelites needed to be pushed in order to be able to give God glory. He knew that those seven days would bring them to their knees, causing them to be stretched, grow, and trust in the Lord in ways that they never had to learn before.

I have a tendency to protect myself when I'm facing a trial of my own. I put up walls around myself in order to make sure that I am guarded against hurt, pain, or disappointment. I've done it a lot in my relationship with the Lord as well— guarding myself when I'm facing a battle, too worried to let go of my control and surrender to the Lord. What if His plan is entirely different than mine? What

if He wants me to march for seven days instead of just one? Sometimes waking up in the morning and knowing I have to keep going feels impossible. But what I'm learning is that God knows exactly what it's going to take to break the walls down and bring me to my knees, absolutely surrendered to Him and advancing straight ahead.

If you are facing your own battle today, I am with you. I get it. Sometimes the hard work can feel like too much. But I want you to know that as you keep marching around those walls, God is there with you, holding that trumpet, winning that battle for you. He is breaking that wall down brick by brick. Keep walking, keep trusting, keep opening yourself up to the Lord. And when those walls come crashing down and the gates burst open and it's time for you to move forward, keep shouting your praises and giving glory to the One who breaks every brick down for you. Those "seven days" might feel like an incredibly long journey, but God is sovereign every single step of the way as you put one foot in front of the other. The victory is His.

THE VICTORY IS HIS.

Prayer

Lord, You are my trumpet blower. You have taught me how to fight battles on my knees, surrendering to You the entire time. You give me the strength to keep marching, even when I've built up walls to protect myself. Thank You for giving me the strength and courage to keep moving forward. Help me continue to put one foot in front of the other. Thank You for blowing the trumpets of life for me.

Amen.

EVERYTHING HE HAD SPOKEN CAME TRUE.

He Is Our Promise Keeper

the LORD gave to Israel all the land He had sworn to give their
ncestors, and they took possession of it and settled there.
And the LORD gave them rest on every side, just as He had
solemnly promised their ancestors. None of their enemies
could stand against them, for the LORD helped them
conquer all their enemies. Not a single one of all
the good promises the LORD had given to the
family of Israel was left unfulfilled; everything
He had spoken came true.

JOSHUA 21:43-45 NLT

He Is Our Promise Keeper

As an adult, I've had to learn the hard way multiple times that I have to be very careful when promising a child something. Trust me when I say that my kids will latch on to that promise very tightly and hold me to it every chance they can get. Whether it's ice cream for dessert or a trip to Disneyland, kids just don't let you forget, do they? I hate to admit it, but I'm still kind of like that. If you tell me there's a free gift with purchase, I want my free gift! And if you don't follow through with it, I'm going to say you went back on your word! Tell me I'm not the only one.

Have you ever had a period in your life when you started to doubt all of God's promises? Maybe you questioned everything or you just couldn't bring yourself to actually believe what He promises is real. I have been there. To be honest, it wasn't too long ago when I just couldn't connect the dots anymore and truly didn't think God meant any of the things He had promised to me—mostly the promise that He would take care of me no matter what. It wasn't any-

thing God had done that led me to this place of doubting. It was just one disappointment after another. One too many hurts, heartaches, bad choices, and dark, lonely days. After a while, my heart became extremely resentful toward life in general, and I became closed off and unsure if there was any room for God anymore. Why would I give someone my time and my devotion if I wasn't convinced they would do the same in return?

Over and over again, for months and months, in my mind I would question everything I had ever believed of God. There were some days when I was angry at the Lord, shaking my fist at him, wondering why He had let me down or why He had let life get this difficult. There were other days that I would lie in my bed in a tearful silence, wondering why He had forgotten about me. I eventually realized that I couldn't keep living like this. It was wreaking havoc on my life. But I would have to get to a place where I believed in God's promises again, and that was incredibly scary. Sometimes promises get broken. I needed to be reminded somehow

that God would not do the same.

So I started asking questions. Just like my kids do when they want to make sure I'm serious about what I say. Except God was a lot more patient with me than I am with them. Because not only is He our promise keeper, He's also extremely patient with our process. Day in and day out, I would ask Him questions. And while God didn't verbally discuss the answers with me, He answered in His own way, which was an overall feeling of His peace canceling out all my doubts, one by one. Sometimes my questions would be angry, like "Why did You let this happen to me, God?" Other times I would simply ask, "God, if I choose to do this Your way and not my own, are You going to take care of me like You say You will?" Slowly but surely, I started believing God's words again. Most likely because His peace continually reassured me that He will absolutely never fail me and will not let me down. After a while, I realized that I was well on the journey back to Him.

I wish I could say that I finally have it all figured out by now, but there have been a few times since then when I've been tempted to let those doubts creep in again. In moments of confusion or fear, I've panicked and asked the Lord, "Will You be taking care of me? I thought You said You'd take care of me!" And like clockwork, God's peace comes rushing back in and reminds me that His promises never, ever fail us. He is so patient with His children, reminding us any time we need it that He will absolutely never leave us or forsake us. It doesn't matter how many times we shake our fists at Him—yelling, kicking, and screaming, God patiently calms us down and steadies us with His love, grace, and mercy. He promises to truly never fail us. There's no limit to how many times we will break our promises to Him, but God will never break His promises to us. I will be eternally grateful for that and always in awe of who He is and all that He has done for me.

HiS PRoMiSeS TRULY NeVeR FaiL US.

Prayer

Lord, You are my promise keeper.
Today, when any doubts creep into
my mind, strengthen my faith so that
I am able to trust in You and all Your
promises. You have never failed me, and
You have always taken care of me. Thank
You that no matter how many times I've
broken my promises to You, You never
break Your promises to me. Thank You
for being patient with me as I learn.

Amen.

Your faith has saved you.

He Is Our Exhale Moment

A woman suffering from bleeding for twelve years, who had spent all she had on doctors and yet could not be healed by any, approached from behind and touched the end of His robe. Instantly her bleeding stopped.

"Who touched Me?" Jesus asked.

When they all denied it, Peter said, "Master, the crowds are hemming You in and pressing against You."

"Someone did touch Me," said Jesus. "I know that power has gone out from Me." When the woman saw that she was discovered, she came trembling and fell down before Him. In the presence of all the people, she declared the reason she had touched Him and how she was instantly healed. "Daughter," He said to her, "your faith has saved you. Go in peace."

LUKE 8:43-48 CSB

He Is Our Exhale Moment

I have some friends that I will often meet up with after a long day. Usually, one of us will reach out and request to hang out with each other when we need a short breather from work, parenting, or life in general. I call it my "exhale." These are safe friends; they know and love the real me. Usually when I walk toward that table, I find myself holding my breath from all that's been going on during the day. When I finally sit down, I can exhale. I can share all that is going on in my world and listen to all they've got going on in theirs, and we still love each other. We see each other. Is there anything better than being seen? I have learned that it is very important to really see someone and really hear someone. It makes the other person feel valued and known. And all of us have a desire to feel known.

Jesus sees us. We don't have to wait for our exhale moment; He IS our exhale moment. He looks into the deepest parts of who we are and what we're walking through, and He sees it.

He knows the joys, the heartaches, the grief, the sin, the exhaustion. We can be ourselves here.

One of the stories that helps me understand this characteristic of Jesus the most is when He felt the woman touch Him in the crowd. Listen, I hate crowds. I get major anxiety when I'm in a crowded area where too many people are in the same place. Elevators, subways, sporting events, long lines at the grocery store—I stop functioning well. I would venture to say that the crowds that followed Jesus were jam-packed with people desperate to be in His presence. You know how it goes—everyone is trying to get to the front, and people are pushing and shoving and cutting in front of you. I can almost picture it in that moment. And then out of nowhere, Jesus says, "Who touched My clothes?"

He felt the one small touch that needed Him the most. This woman had hemorrhaged and bled for twelve years. *Twelve*. She heard about Jesus, that He might heal her. And all she

wanted was just a small touch of His clothes. So she pushed through that crowd, touched the bottom of His cloak, and Jesus felt her. Peter pointed out that it was crowded, and people were pressing on Jesus. Maybe Jesus had been mistaken? But He knew that someone had touched His cloak in order to be healed. He stopped what He was doing and looked around the crowd and *He saw the woman*. Jesus healed her instantly, and she sensed it in her body—the bleeding had ceased. I'm sure she'd held her breath the entire way as she pushed through that crowd, and this was it—her exhale moment. Jesus had seen her.

Doesn't it feel good to feel known? We all need those people whom we let in to really see and know us. To be our exhale moment at the end of a long day, week, or season. To be able to let our guards down and our shoulders relax as we push our way through the crowded thoughts in our busy minds. I'm so glad we don't have to wait for that moment with Jesus. He is always

right there, seeing our hand reach for His cloak when we are desperately in need of His comfort, healing, and presence in our lives. Is there anything better?

You can stop holding your breath today. Jesus is right there, waiting for you to exhale.

Prayer

Jesus, thank You for being my exhale moment, the One who truly sees me for all that I am and all that I'm walking through today. Lord, I need strength to remember that I am known by You, fully known. I can be myself with You and let my guard down. On days when that is easily forgotten for me, please let me feel Your presence, like the sick woman felt Your touch. I'm so thankful for You.

Amen.

Be joyful always.

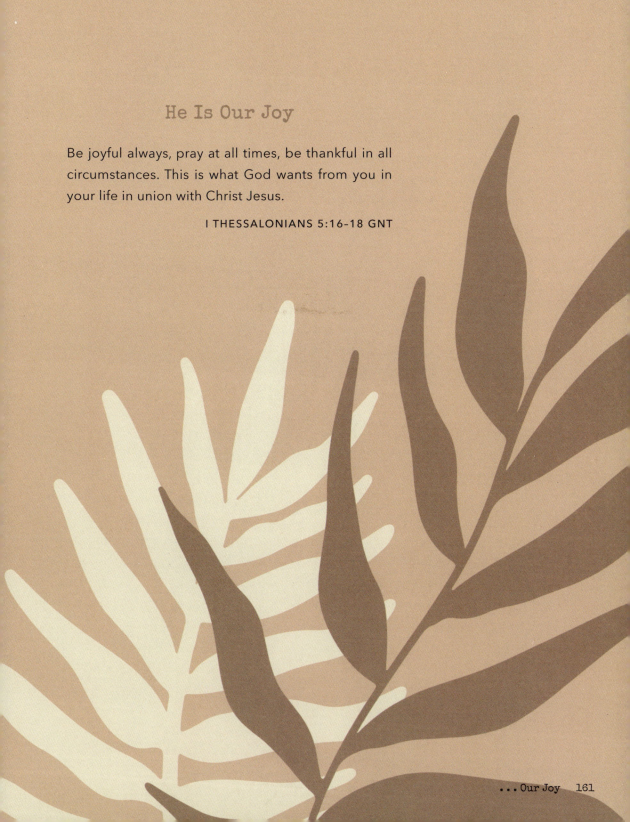

He Is Our Joy

Be joyful always, pray at all times, be thankful in all circumstances. This is what God wants from you in your life in union with Christ Jesus.

I THESSALONIANS 5:16-18 GNT

He Is Our Joy

A nd don't forget to smile during the entire sixty-second sprint!" my instructor yelled during the running class I take on my treadmill. My head jerked up as I stared at this woman telling me to smile while I was running. Was she out of her mind? I do not like to work out. In fact, daily I will find every excuse not to lace up my shoes and press start on my machine. But I've learned how important exercise is for me personally. It is good for my body, my mind, and my soul. But I am not a runner. It's something I have to work very hard at, and it does not come naturally for me. And I absolutely do not smile while I'm doing it! I'm pretty much begging for mercy. But the instructor went on to explain to us that smiling while running would actually help us run faster and harder while simultaneously bringing us joy. Smiling would help us persevere through the run and give us strength to endure it.

Pause for a moment and think about a time in your life when you tried your best to keep smiling through a difficult time. Have you ever been around someone who exudes joy in the Lord? I notice it a lot when people are worshipping together. When I see someone singing the words to Jesus through a huge smile on their face, their joy is contagious to me. I want what they're having. It's hard to remember sometimes that underneath that smile there may be something really difficult going on that they're having to endure. And sometimes we just have the joy of the Lord flowing out of us because we simply cannot contain it.

Joy is defined as a feeling of great pleasure and happiness. I don't know about you, but when I start to think—really think—about all that the Lord has done for me and all that He has saved me from, I can't help but feel that way. I cannot help but smile. When I start thinking about who God is in my life, tears of joy easily fill my eyes and talking is difficult because of the lump in my throat. I get chills on my body; I get a bounce in my step. My heart starts beating faster, and I breathe a lot easier when I start thinking about God and what His presence does to me. Having joy in the Lord changes who I am and how I live my life every day.

There are a lot of moments when I have not chosen joy and have not chosen to keep smiling through the pain. I have chosen darkness, depression, anger, bitterness—anything other than actual joy. I have found every excuse in the book to grumble and complain through a difficult time instead of letting the joy of the Lord flow through me. It is so much harder that way, and I am so much weaker when I go that route. Nehemiah 8:10 (CSB) says, "The joy of the LORD is your strength." His joy literally makes us stronger. When we slow down and open our hands to the Lord in surrender and worship, and we actively choose to search for the joy of the Lord in everything we do, it becomes easier and easier to find it. My running instructor told us that the more we smile during our exercises, the more it becomes habitual and the easier the run gets. I think that's true for joy as well. The more we choose joy in the Lord, the more it becomes a natural experience for us and the more it flows from our hearts.

God has given us so much to be joyful about! We can walk a little lighter, breathe a little deeper, and smile more than we ever have. His joy is our strength.

Prayer

Dear Jesus, thank You for giving me the strength to keep smiling no matter what my circumstances are. Your strength makes me stronger. I pray that whatever comes my way today, I will be able to find my joy in You. Thank You for changing who I am with Your joy and how I live my life every day.

Amen.

Slow down
and remember...

Let us hold tightly
without wavering
to the hope we
affirm, for God
can be trusted
to keep his
promise.

Hebrews 10:23 NLT

the flour jar will Not become empty + the oil jug will Not Run dry.

He Is Our Provider

So Elijah got up and went to Zarephath. When he arrived at the city gate, there was a widow gathering wood. Elijah called to her and said, "Please bring me a little water in a cup and let me drink." As she went to get it, he called to her and said, "Please bring me a piece of bread in your hand."

But she said, "As the LORD your God lives, I don't have anything baked— only a handful of flour in the jar and a bit of oil in the jug. Just now, I am gathering a couple of sticks in order to go prepare it for myself and my son so we can eat it and die."

Then Elijah said to her, "Don't be afraid; go and do as you have said. But first make me a small loaf from it and bring it out to me. Afterward, you may make some for yourself and your son, for this is what the LORD God of Israel says, 'The flour jar will not become empty and the oil jug will not run dry until the day the Lord sends rain on the surface of the land.'"

I KINGS 17:10-14 CSB

He Is Our Provider

Sometimes I pray for funny things. Like if I pull into the Target parking lot and it seems crowded, I'll pray that God will let a front-row parking space open up for me. Or sometimes when I'm walking to the mailbox, I'll pray that there will be a fun surprise in there for me because I love mail so much. I've prayed that my kids would win their soccer games—I bet that one makes God laugh. And the one that makes me cringe deep down in the depths of my soul: in college, when I had a huge, massive crush on my now husband, I prayed that God would give me signs to show me that Scott shared the same feelings. And then I would search high and low for those signs and hold on as tightly as I could to anything even remotely close. I definitely roll my eyes at myself when I think about that now. So embarrassing! The thing that I love about this fun fact about me is that so many times God has given me the parking spot. And I get giddy like a little kid on Christmas morning because I just believe it was a little message from the Lord that He remembers me and that He's providing for me.

What about when we pray for the "big" things though? We've all been there, praying for God to provide for us in a miraculous way. Maybe we've lost our job, or we're tired of being single, or we're desperate for a baby and can't get pregnant. Maybe we can't make ends meet this month or we need the chemotherapy to work this time around. Maybe we're just swimming upstream and we need the strength to make it through today. Sometimes we are desperate for God's provision and we are hoping, praying, and trusting for an actual miracle. It takes a lot of faith to trust that He's going to provide for us even if His plan and timing are different than ours.

I came across a story of Elijah and a widow in I Kings chapter 17. There had been a drought and a famine going on in Israel for three years at that point, so food was scarce and discouragement was high. The Lord had sent Elijah on a journey throughout the land, and he told Elijah there was a widow and her son waiting to house him there. When Elijah arrived, he asked the woman for some water and a piece of bread. But

the widow told him that she had only enough flour in her jar for one more meal, very little oil left in her jug, and then she and her son would die—from starvation. Elijah told the woman that her flour jar would not become empty and the oil jug would not run dry until the Lord sent rain to the land. God would not allow the widow and her son to starve. She would always have enough.

God will always provide a way for us. I know the worst-case scenario often seems to be the first thought in our minds, but God is not going to leave us high and dry. Our responsibility is to have faith that God will continue to take care of us. The widow had to trust that what Elijah told her was the truth—that God would not leave her and her son hungry. She had to put her faith in the Lord and believe that He would provide food and water for her household. And you know what? God did. Sometimes when we're waiting on the Lord for something, we do like I did when I prayed for a sign that Scott was the one—we grasp for anything we can to show us the answers or to calm

our hearts down, but we forget to be still and trust that He's taking care of us. God's way of providing might not always look like what we have in mind. His timing and His means are often far different than ours. We want answers to fall from the sky like manna; He wants us to trust in His perfect plan. God kept His promises and He provided for the widow. Just as God will keep His promises and continue to provide for you and me.

Maybe next time we get a front-row spot in a busy parking lot, we'll be reminded of the story of the widow and her son and give thanks for the Lord for all the ways He's continuing to show up for us.

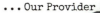

HIS JOY IS OUR STRENGTH.

Prayer

Lord, You are my provider. You performed miracle after miracle in Your Word where You provided in a time of need. I know that Your timing and Your ways are oftentimes not what I would choose for myself, but You are strengthening my faith and helping me trust in Your perfect plan for my life. Thank You for never leaving me empty, Jesus, but always making sure I'm taken care of. I put my faith in You.

Amen.

His glory fills the world.

He Is Glory

In the year that King Uzziah died, I saw the Lord. He was sitting on His throne, high and exalted, and His robe filled the whole Temple. Around Him flaming creatures were standing, each of which had six wings. Each creature covered its face with two wings, and its body with two, and used the other two for flying. They were calling out to each other:

"Holy, holy, holy!
The LORD Almighty is holy!
His glory fills the world."

ISAIAH 6:1–3 GNT

He Is Glory

I've been hearing the story of David and Goliath since I was a little girl. I am sure I brought home at least five Sunday school crafts showing the story of a boy defeating a giant. And now as an adult, we hear the story in sermons. A lot of them. It's a great story! It teaches us to face our fears and defeat our giants with God on our side. I thought I couldn't learn anything else about this Bible passage because I had heard it so many times. Until I read it recently. Just when we think God has taught us everything about a certain topic, He goes and blows our minds and teaches us more.

When I read the story this time around, I didn't hear one word about fear. Yes, I'm sure David was afraid to battle it out with a huge giant like Goliath. But I didn't read that in I Samuel 17 this time. I thought I had this story all figured out! To be honest, Goliath seemed more afraid than David. I mean, he wore 125 pounds' worth of armor, and then a shield bearer walked in front of him. That's a lot of armor for someone who seemed so gigantically fearless. When David put on his armor, he immediately asked to take it off. He couldn't walk right, and he wasn't used to how it all felt. So he just packed five stones in a pouch and approached Goliath.

I would be absolutely shaking if it were me. But David seemed very confident that he would win this battle—because he knew the battle belonged to the Lord. David told Goliath that he would strike him down, and THEN all the world would know that Israel has a God. David knew in his heart that he would win this battle because it would bring God glory and His name would be proclaimed to all the world. And THAT is why David did what he did. He didn't do it for popularity, which I'm sure he obtained. He didn't do it for a medal or anything like that. He defeated Goliath so that Israel would know there was a God. I mean, think about it! We are still talking about David and Goliath to this day! God won that battle for David, God defeated Goliath, and God deserved all the glory.

Awhile back, I faced my own battle, my own giant. I mean, I guess I've faced a lot of them—sometimes I've walked myself right into these battles because of really poor choices I've made. But this one seemed particularly difficult. I felt like I would wake up not understanding how I was going to even make it through the day. I decided to pray one day that I would go through whatever God wanted me to go through as long as His name was proclaimed and His glory was revealed in the end. That's a very scary prayer to pray. And let me tell you, it was hard. Every day felt hard during that period of time. I had to humbly trust that God was going to do

what God does and win that battle for me. And you know what? He did, just as He always does. In the end, God's name was and still is proclaimed and His glory is still revealed.

Whatever battle you're facing today, whether you're walking into it with worry like I did or confidence like David did, the battle is the Lord's. Let the world know that you have a God, and wait until His glory is revealed through whatever you're facing.

god deserved all the glory.

Prayer

Lord, You alone are worthy of all glory. Thank You for the story of David and Goliath to teach me how to fight my battles to bring You glory in the end. I pray that Your name is proclaimed through me every day. Continue to show me Your glory every step of the way, through everything I face. You are worthy of it all.

Amen.

god's loyal love couldn't have run out.

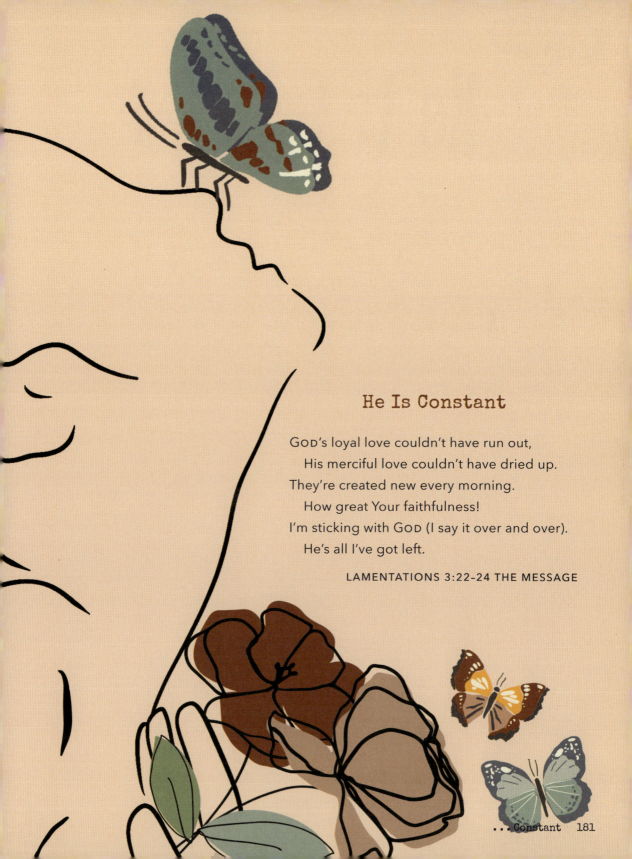

He Is Constant

GOD's loyal love couldn't have run out,
  His merciful love couldn't have dried up.
They're created new every morning.
  How great Your faithfulness!
I'm sticking with GOD (I say it over and over).
  He's all I've got left.

LAMENTATIONS 3:22-24 THE MESSAGE

He Is Constant

Do you have a constant friend? Someone who stands by your side at all times, no matter what? The older I get, the more I realize how difficult it is to find one. Women are fickle. We can be very insecure, critical, and jealous. Gossip is a really easy thing to turn to in moments like that. I didn't meet my best friend, Brooke, until I was twenty-two. And she has been my most constant friend for the last twenty years. The tricky part is that I live in California, and she lives in Virginia. Every day there are 2,723.5 miles between us, so we've had to learn how to make it work. We've lived life together under countless different skies. We've stood beside each other on our wedding days; we've walked through conflict and resolution, death and grief, births and adoptions, joys and heartaches. We've shared a million deep conversations on the front porches of life, with twinkle lights, Dr Peppers, and chips and salsa. There is no one quite like Brooke. I've learned that friendships come and go, but she has been a constant in my life.

But as much as Brooke has been a part of my life, she doesn't always answer my texts at the exact moment I need her. I also can't call her up and hang out at the end of a long day, since she's across the country. I can't expect her to be there every time something big happens in my life, and I'm certainly not able to be at her side all the time either. That's because no matter how deep our friendship goes or how loyal we are to each other, we are human and life just doesn't work that way. There is only One that is truly constant in our lives.

If you step back and think about it, we never have to wonder what to expect from Jesus. There's no rocky mountain to climb or holding on tight when we're going over rolling waves. There's no wondering if He's going to accept us today or wondering what kind of mood He'll be in. He's not going to reject us, silence us, or skip out on our most important moments. His feelings toward us never waver, even when we do. Jesus is constant. So throughout every high and every low, no matter what we're going through, Jesus is still

on His throne, always staying the same in a world that seems to be changing by the minute.

That's something I need reminding of often: that no matter what changes around us, Jesus is still on His throne.

When we're breaking down and feel like we aren't going to make it, Jesus is still on His throne.

When our biggest dreams have come true and we're walking on cloud nine, Jesus is still on His throne.

When it feels like the storms are going to last forever, Jesus is still on His throne.

When darkness feels like it's closing in on you and there's no way out, Jesus is still on His throne.

When you're so filled with joy that you can't help the songs escaping your mouth, Jesus is still on His throne.

Jesus is steadfast. We can trust that He will never fail us. He is not tempted to change. He tells us exactly that in Malachi 3:6 (CSB): "Because I, the LORD, have not changed." When facing a trial of any kind, I lose sight of this pretty much immediately. Why do I always

forget this? I start freaking out and panicking and jumping to the worst-case scenario. But even then, Jesus is still the same. Still our constant and still on His throne.

I need this reminder for myself often, so it helps me to make a list. Whether my heart is filled with joy or sorrow, worry or peace, contentment or angst, it's so helpful to recognize that God's presence in my life is constant. I don't even have to travel 2,723.5 miles to get to Him! So today if you're needing your own reminder, grab a piece of paper and start jotting down the ways in your life that you've come to realize Jesus is still on His throne, no matter what. Maybe the more we remind ourselves, the more we'll see Him, and the list will keep growing every day.

Prayer

Lord, there is only one person who will never fail me and that is You. Thank You, Jesus, for being so steadfast in my life, for being a loving Savior we can always count on—in both the famine and the feast. You never change; You always stay the same. Thank You for being constant. You are always on Your throne no matter what.

Amen.

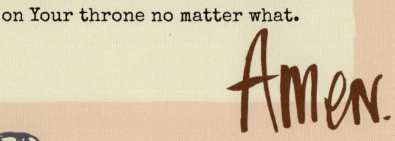

There's more joy in Heaven over one sinner's Rescued Life

He Is Our Shepherd

Suppose one of you had a hundred sheep and lost one. Wouldn't you leave the ninety-nine in the wilderness and go after the lost one until you found it? When found, you can be sure you would put it across your shoulders, rejoicing, and when you got home call in your friends and neighbors, saying, "Celebrate with me! I've found my lost sheep!" Count on it—there's more joy in heaven over one sinner's rescued life than over ninety-nine good people in no need of rescue."

LUKE 15:4–7 THE MESSAGE

He Is Our Shepherd

Scott proposed to me in a quaint little town outside of London called Woolacombe. It is the cutest little beach town, and he walked me out onto this cliff overlooking the ocean. I would love to show you pictures of it, but the day after the proposal, we left our camera on a double-decker bus, never to be seen again. But that is beside the point, and the memories of that special moment are all captured perfectly like snapshots in my mind. It was wonderful. There was a lighthouse, rolling green hills, and a lot of . . . sheep. There were sheep everywhere, actually. I took notice of them because I thought they were so beautiful. They fit in well with the scenery as they were just roaming around, doing their own thing, with no rhyme or reason. Looking back, as pretty as those sheep were, I remember wondering where they came from. They seemed to just be on their own.

I think I notice sheep a lot because my mom had them all over our house in the nineties. My eyes just gravitate toward them. My mom and I both love to decorate our homes, so I think it must have been a huge trend back then. She even had an entire bathroom wallpapered with some sort of trendy sheep wallpaper. I recently asked why she decorated with them so much when I was little. Her response: "Well, the Bible says we're like sheep. And if you've ever read about sheep, they're very dumb. One of them does something, and the rest follow. They wander, and they need a shepherd to guide them; otherwise they don't follow orders, and they just run off." Kind of like the sheep on that cliff in Woolacombe. Just wandering for no reason.

The Bible does talk a lot about shepherds and sheep. We really are a lot like those cute yet odd animals. Sheep are easily distracted, easily enticed, and prone to wander in areas that just aren't safe. Sounds . . . familiar. Honestly, all the ways sheep are described reminds me so much of myself that it's hard to be offended that God uses sheep to compare us to so often. I lose my footing all the time, following the wrong crowd on the wrong path, only to get lost and realize I've just wandered so far from the straight road I should have just stayed on in the beginning.

We all carry the characteristics of sheep in our own way. Some of us choose to wander and make our own dumb decisions that lead us away from the Shepherd. And some of us are easily distracted by enticing situations, and all of a sudden, we're in green grass two fields over with no clue how we ended up there. Some of us are both. I'd venture to say that sheep don't have it all figured out yet either.

However, here's what I love so much about Jesus, our own personal Shepherd. He says in Luke 15:4 (CSB), "What man among you, who has a hundred sheep and loses one of them, does not leave the ninety-nine in the open field and go after the lost one until he finds it?" I love this so much because out of those one hundred sheep, not one was more important than the other. Jesus didn't point out that the sheep that went missing was the worst one. He didn't call out his mistakes or list why he went off the beaten path. He

just gave the facts. That if there are one hundred sheep and one goes missing, the shepherd has no problem leaving the other ninety-nine in the open field to go after the lost one until he finds it. He doesn't give up and call it a night after he searches for an hour. He looks until he finds the missing sheep. I can't tell you how relieving that is, because I've been that missing sheep so many times in my life.

The story doesn't end there though. Jesus goes on to say that when the shepherd finds the sheep, he *joyfully* puts it on his shoulders and calls his friends and neighbors over to rejoice with him now that the missing sheep is found. He's not frustrated at the extra work or expressing annoyance at the detours of the day. He is filled with so much joy that the missing sheep is found.

He Leaves the Ninety-Nine.

Prayer

Lord, You are my Shepherd. You have chosen over and over again to go running after Your children who have lost their way, like me. You chase after us until You find us. I love that once You find Your missing sheep, You joyfully put it on Your shoulders and rejoice. Lord, thank You for guiding me and protecting me. Thank You for never giving up on me when I've taken a wrong turn. I love You.

Amen.

THERE is NO
OTHER GOD
WHO is ABLE
to deLiVER
LiKE THiS.

He Is Our Plus-One

Nebuchadnezzar exclaimed, "Praise to the God of Shadrach, Meshach, and Abednego! He sent His angel and rescued His servants who trusted in Him. They violated the king's command and risked their lives rather than serve or worship any god except their own God. Therefore I issue a decree that anyone of any people, nation, or language who says anything offensive against the God of Shadrach, Meshach, and Abednego will be torn limb from limb and his house made a garbage dump. For there is no other god who is able to deliver like this.

DANIEL 3:24-25 CSB

He Is Our Plus One

Scott and I woke up one morning with a list a mile long of weights we carried. Between the two of us, there was conflict with a friend, deadlines for my job, heavy work stress for his, a hard conversation on the horizon, life decisions that needed to be made, and kids that both had their own troubles going on. It was a lot. It felt like a lot. Ever have one of those days? He went for a run, and I got my morning coffee, opened my Bible, and prayed. It was all I knew to do. And as I started praying, bringing everything that was on my mind to the feet of Jesus, I felt this reminder nudging me that we would not be alone in anything we faced today. No matter what fires came our way, we would not walk through them on our own. The Lord would be beside us for every one. We hear that a lot: "God will never leave your side." It's an excellent reminder and a perfect thing to say in order to encourage someone. It makes perfect wall art and a perfect greeting card when you can't find the right words on your own. It's truth—God actually will never leave our side—but when we have to put our faith to the test

with those six small words, it changes everything. It takes a very strong person to walk through the daily battles of life believing God is never leaving us.

Shadrach, Meshach, and Abednego. I mean, those guys had to have some of the strongest faith we've read about in the Bible, you know? Daniel 3 tells their story. King Nebuchadnezzar had made a gold statue ninety feet tall and ninety feet wide. That is a lot of gold. And out of nowhere, he just decided that at any given moment in the day, music could be played and every person of every nation would need to fall facedown and worship this massive gold situation. And if you didn't, you'd be thrown into a furnace of blazing fire immediately. This guy seemed like a fun guy, right?

Enter Shadrach, Meshach, and Abednego. Their faith didn't lie in a gigantic gold statue, their faith was in the Lord and only the Lord. And despite the fear of being thrown into the furnace—I mean, can you even imagine?—they had absolute certainty that God would never leave their side. So they did not bow down. They would rather die in a fire than obey

the king's demands and serve false gods. They stood strong and had faith that serving the Most High was truly the only way, even if they had to die. Nebuchadnezzar was furious. He gave orders immediately to heat the furnace up seven times what was normal. And he had his soldiers literally throw Shadrach, Meshach, and Abednego into that blazing fire. The flames were so violent and so hot that the soldiers who carried them died immediately.

And as Nebuchadnezzar watched, he realized that there were no longer three bodies in the fiery furnace. There were four. There was another in the fire with them. God did not leave their side, just as He has promised us. The king called Shadrach, Meshach, and Abednego out of the fire, and they walked out with not even one hair singed, not even the smell of fire on them. God had absolutely saved their lives! What a testament of faith and what a beautiful miracle.

Listen, I don't know what kind of fires you are facing today. Maybe you're dealing with your own gold statues. I get it. I have mine too. And sometimes

life is just plain hard. But this morning Jesus reminded me that I would not be alone today, and He's doing the same for you. Following Jesus means we get a plus-one. He never leaves our side, and He does not let us walk through any of those fires alone.

Nebuchadnezzar ends the story of Shadrach, Meshach, and Abednego by saying this: "There is no other god who is able to deliver like this." And he's right. There is no one else like Jesus. So thankful there's another in the fire with us today.

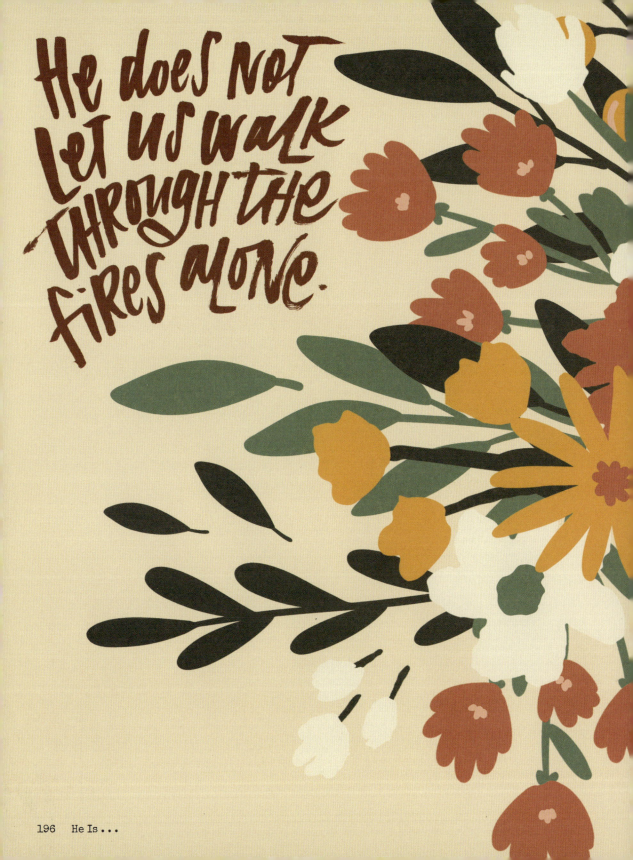

He does not let us walk through the fires alone.

Prayer

Thank You, Jesus, that You walk
through the fires of life with me.
Thank You that on the hard days, You
are reminding me that I am not alone.
You are my plus-one. Help strengthen
my faith on the days when I forget that
You're never leaving my side. You have
been so faithful to me, Jesus. Thank
You for all You have done for me.

Amen.

Breathe in
these truths...

God, create a
clean heart
for me and renew
a steadfast
spirit within me.

Psalm 51:10 CSB

FROM THE RISING OF THE SUN TO ITS SETTING

He Is Our Pink Skies

Hallelujah!
Give praise, servants of the LORD;
praise the name of the LORD.
Let the name of the LORD be blessed
both now and forever.
From the rising of the sun to its setting,
let the name of the LORD be praised.
The LORD is exalted above all the nations,
His glory above the heavens.
Who is like the LORD our God—
the one enthroned on high,
who stoops down to look
on the heavens and the earth?

PSALM 113:1-6 CSB

He Is Our Pink Skies

I wish I could describe to you what pink skies mean to me. I've always been a sunset lover. I have this secret spot I go to when I want to watch the sun set over the horizon. It just does something to me. It calms me—my busy mind, my spinning heart, and my weary soul. I start anticipating the whole adventure, the rays extending across the skies, the clouds turning color, the sun making its presence known until the very last sliver gets lost. I wait, holding my breath, to see how the skies will change from blue to yellow to orange and then—my very favorite—pink. There is nothing quite like a pink sky. I sit there in silence, watching, waiting, processing, and pondering. And then I allow peace to slowly wash over me when the time finally arrives that the Lord captivates my attention with His beautiful masterpiece once again. In those moments, I am finally still. I am taking everything in. Every color, every hue, every different and new way the sky is transforming. The skies turn magical, and the clouds look like strokes from my favorite paintbrush. I am a different person in the presence of a pink sunset. It is everything.

This is what Jesus feels like to me. He is my pink sky. He is in every ray of light that spans across my life. He is the color in every cloud that hangs over my head. He allows His presence to be made known and captivates every ounce of awe I'm able to understand. He is my peace in the midst of chaos and my calm in the midst of storm. He is strong and steady like the rising and the setting of the sun. He has changed me into a new person, and He continues to mold me into someone more like Him with every passing day. He is everything to me.

For thirty-one chapters, I have poured out the deepest parts of my soul onto these pages. Thirty-one ways I have rediscovered the Lord and all of His glory have been laid out in this book. The mistakes I've made, the darkness I've experienced, and the promises I've forgotten and have had to relearn. I thought I'd have it all figured out by

now, but you know what? In some ways, as I've written this book, I've learned it's supposed to be this way. We are never going to fully arrive until we meet Jesus face-to-face. We just keep learning. We keep growing and changing, little by little, inch by inch. Just like the sky at dusk.

I wish we could watch the sunset together. Because if we were sitting side by side, waiting in anticipation for the sky to do its glorious thing, I'd tell you that you're seen. I'd share with you that you can be yourself here, just exactly who God made you to be. I'd tell you I know what it's like to walk with shame, insecurity, worry, grief, heartache, messy floors, and messy life, so you're in good company with me. I'd tell you that I don't have it all together either, but I am learning more and more every day about what following Jesus looks like in a world like ours.

We were created for one purpose—to bring Him glory. Tears are filling my eyes as I'm writing this because honestly, that is all I want for my life—

to bring Him glory. Jesus is everything to me. And I've learned so much more about Him while on the journey of writing the pages in this book. While neither of us have it all together or all figured out by now, we have one thing: Jesus. He is who He says He is, and that is enough for us. Our pink skies. He is worthy of all our praise.

He is in every ray of light.

Prayer

Jesus, You have taken me on a journey these last thirty-one days to rediscover You and all that You are to me. I pray that You will continue to stretch me and grow me into someone who seeks You with everything I am. You are my everything; You are all that I want and need. All I want in this life is to bring You glory, Father. Allow Your presence to wash over me like the sunset, changing who I am and making me more like You. You never change, and You never break Your promises. You are exactly who You say You are, Jesus. I love You.

Amen.

Katy Fults is a self-taught hand letterer and author who is well-known for her beautifully drawn, affirming messages of God's hope, joy, and unconditional love. In addition to a large social media following and her thriving Katygirl Designs online business, Katy's original style can also be found in her prints, cards, books, and calendars available in retailers across the United States. She lives with her husband, Scott, and two beautiful children, Miles and Camden, in Bakersfield, California.

Dear Friend,

This book was prayerfully crafted with you, the reader, in mind. Every word, every sentence, every page was thoughtfully written, designed, and packaged to encourage you—right where you are this very moment. At DaySpring, our vision is to see every person experience the life-changing message of God's love. So, as we worked through rough drafts, design changes, edits, and details, we prayed for you to deeply experience His unfailing love, indescribable peace, and pure joy. It is our sincere hope that through these Truth-filled pages your heart will be blessed, knowing that God cares about you—your desires and disappointments, your challenges and dreams.

He knows. He cares. He loves you unconditionally.

BLESSINGS!
THE DAYSPRING BOOK TEAM

**Additional copies of this book and
other DaySpring titles can be purchased
at fine retailers everywhere.
Order online at dayspring.com
or
by phone at 1-877-751-4347**